1.21 GIGAWATT EDITION

LIMITED TO 1,000 PRINTS

★ ★ ★ GRAYS ★ ★ ★

SPORTS

ALMANAC

COMPLETE SPORTS STATISTICS

1950–2000

STATISTICS

1950

1950 NATIONAL FOOTBALL LEAGUE SEASON STANDINGS

AMERICAN	W	T	L	NATIONAL	W	L	T
Cleveland	10	2	0	Los Angeles	9	3	0
NY Giants	10	2	0	Chi. Bears	9	3	0
Philadelphia	6	6	0	NY Yanks	7	5	0
Pittsburgh	6	6	0	Detroit	6	6	0
Chi. Cardinals	5	7	0	Green Bay	3	9	0
Washington	3	9	0				

1950 U.S NATIONAL BADMINTON CHAMPIONSHIPS WINNER

Mens Singles	Womens Singles	Mens Doubles	Womens Doubles	Mixed Doubles
Marten Mendez	Ether Marshall	Barney McCay Wynn Rogers	Thelma Scovil Janet Wright	Wynn Rogers Loma Moulton

1950 NBA STANDINGS DIVISION STANDINGS

Team	W	L	W/L%	GB	PS/G	PA/G	SRS
Central Division							
Minneapolis Lakers	51	17	0.750	---	84.1	75.7	8.25
Rochester Royals	51	17	0.750	---	82.4	74.6	7.72
Fort Wayne Pistons	40	28	0.588	11.0	79.3	77.9	1.84
Chicago Stags	40	28	0.588	11.0	78.7	77.1	2.06
St. Louis Bombers	26	42	0.382	25.0	73.7	76.5	-2.01
Eastern Division							
Syracuse Nationals	51	13	0.797	---	84.8	76.7	6.48
New York Knicks	40	28	0.588	13	80.7	78.6	2.53
Washington Capitols	32	36	0.471	21	76.5	77.4	-0.28
Philadelphia Warriors	26	42	0.382	27	73.3	76.4	-2.27
Baltimore Bullets	25	43	0.368	28	73.1	78.7	-4.55
Boston Celtics	22	46	0.324	31	79.7	82.2	-1.73
Western Division							
Indianapolis Olympians	39	25	0.609	---	85.8	82.1	2.59
Anderson Packers	37	27	0.578	2	87.3	83.5	2.42
Tri-Cities Black Hawks	29	35	0.453	10	83	83.6	2.42
Sheboygan Red Skins	22	40	0.355	16	82.4	87.8	-5.85
Waterloo Hawks	19	43	0.306	19	79.4	84.9	-5.96
Denver Nuggets	11	15	0.177	27	77.7	89.2	-11.31

AMERICAN HORSE OF THE YEAR
1950 ECLIPSE REWARD

Horse	Trainer	Owner	Age	Gender
Hill Prince	Casey Hayes	Christopher Chenery	3	C

1950 NHL SEASON
FINAL STANDINGS

National Hockey Height	GP	W	L	T	Pts	GF	GA	PIM
Detroit Red Wings	70	44	13	13	101	236	139	566
Toronto Maple Leafs	70	41	16	13	95	212	138	823
Montreal Canadiens	70	25	30	15	65	173	184	835
Boston Bruins	70	22	30	18	62	178	197	656
New York Rangers	70	20	29	21	61	169	201	774
Chicago Black Hawks	70	13	47	10	36	171	280	615

1950 MAJOR LEAGUE BASEBALL SEASON HISTORY

1950 American League Standings

TEAM	W	L	PCT	GB	HOME	ROAD	RS	RA	DIFF
New York	98	56	0.632	---	---	---	914	691	+223
Detroit	95	59	.605	3	---	---	837	713	+124
Boston	94	60	.610	4	---	---	1027	804	+223
Cleveland	92	62	.594	6	---	---	806	654	+152
Washington	67	87	.432	31	---	---	690	813	-123
Chicago	60	94	.385	38	---	---	625	749	-124
St. Louis	58	96	.377	40	---	---	684	916	-232
Philadelphia	52	102	.338	46	---	---	670	913	-243

1950 National League Standings

TEAM	W	L	PCT	GB	HOME	ROAD	RS	RA	DIFF
Philadelphia	91	63	.580	---	---	---	722	624	+98
Brooklyn	89	65	.574	2	---	---	847	724	+123
New York	86	68	.558	5	---	---	735	643	+92
Boston	83	71	.532	8	---	---	785	736	+49
St. Louis	78	75	.510	12.5	---	---	693	670	+23
Cincinnati	66	87	.431	24.5	---	---	654	734	-80
Chicago	64	89	.416	26.5	---	---	643	772	-129
Pittsburgh	57	96	.370	33.5	---	---	681	857	-176

1950 U.S NATIONAL TENNIS CHAMPIONSHIPS

Mens Singles – Art Larsen defeated Herb Flam 6-3, 4-6, 5-7, 6-4, 6-3
Womens Singles – Margaret Osborne duPont defeated Doris Hart 6-3, 6-3
Mens Doubles – John Bromwich / Frank Sedgman defeated Bill Talbert / Gardnar Mulloy 7-5, 8-6, 3-6, 6-1
Womens Doubles – Louise Brough / Margaret Osborne defeated Shirley Fry / Doris Hart 6-2, 6-3
Mixed Doubles – Margaret Osborne duPont / Ken McGregor defeated Doris Hart / Frank Sedgman 6-4, 3-6, 6-3

1951

1951 NATIONAL FOOOTBALL LEAGUE SEASON STANDINGS

AMERICAN	W	L	T	NATIONAL	W	L	T
Cleveland	11	1	0	Los Angeles	8	4	0
NY Giants	9	2	1	Detroit	7	4	1
Washington	5	7	0	San Francisco	7	4	1
Pittsburgh	4	7	1	Chi. Bears	7	5	1
Philadelphia	4	8	0	Green Bay	3	9	0
Chi. Cardinals	3	9	0	NY Yanks	1	9	2

1951 U.S NATIONOAL BADMINTON CHAMPIONOSHIPS WINNERS

Mens Singles	Womens Singles	Mens Doubles	Womens Doubles	Mixed Doubles
Joseph Cameron Alston	Ethel Marshall	Joe Alston Wynn Rogers	Dorothy Hann Loma Moulton Smith	Wynn Rogers Loma Moulton Smith

1951 NBA STANDINGS DIVISION STANDINGS

Team	W	L	W/L%	GB	PS/G	PA/G	SRS
Eastern Division							
Philadelphia Warriors	40	26	.606	---	85.4	81.6	3.40
Boston Celtics	39	30	.565	2.5	85.2	85.5	-0.41
New York Knicks	36	30	.545	4.0	85.8	85.4	0.49
Syracuse Nationals	32	34	.485	8.0	86.1	85.5	0.62
Baltimore Bullets	24	42	.364	16.0	82.0	84.3	-1.94
Washington Capitols	10	25	.286	14.5	81.3	86.0	-4.63
Western Division							
Minneapolis Lakers	44	24	.647	---	82.8	77.4	4.79
Rochester Royals	41	27	.603	3.0	84.6	81.7	2.54
Fort Wayne Pistons	32	36	.471	12.0	84.1	86.0	-1.81
Indianapolis Olympians	31	37	.456	13.0	81.7	84.1	-2.00
Tri-Cities Blackhawks	25	43	.368	19.0	84.3	88.1	-3.22

AMERICAN HORSE OF THE YEAR 1951 ECLIPSE YEAR

Horse	Trainer	Owner	Age	Gender
Counterpoint	Sylvester Veitch	C. V. Whitney	3	C

1951 NHL SEASON
FINAL STANDINGS

National Hockey League	GP	W	L	T	Pts	GF	GA	PIM
Detroit Red Wings	70	44	14	12	100	215	133	694
Montreal Canadiens	70	34	26	10	78	195	164	661
Toronto Maple Leafs	70	29	25	16	74	168	157	841
Boston Bruins	70	25	29	16	66	162	176	601
New York Rangers	70	23	34	13	59	192	219	532
Chicago Blackhawks	70	17	44	9	43	158	241	627

1951 MAJOR LEAGUE BASEBALL SEASON HISTORY
1951 American League Standings

TEAM	W	L	PCT	GB	HOME	ROAD	RS	RA	DIFF
New York	98	56	.636	---	---	---	798	621	+177
Cleveland	93	61	.600	5	---	---	696	594	+102
Boston	87	67	.565	11	---	---	804	725	+79
Chicago	81	73	.523	17	---	---	714	644	+70
Detroit	73	81	.474	25	---	---	685	741	-56
Philadelphia	70	84	.455	28	---	---	736	745	-9
Washington	62	92	.403	36	---	---	672	764	-92
St. Louis	52	102	.338	46	---	---	611	882	-271

1951 National League Standing

TEAM	W	L	PCT	GB	HOME	ROAD	RS	RA	DIFF
New York	98	59	.624	---	---	---	781	641	+140
Brooklyn	97	60	.614	1	---	---	855	672	+183
St. Louis	81	73	.523	15.5	---	---	683	671	+12
Boston	76	78	.490	20.5	---	---	723	662	+61
Philadelphia	73	81	.474	23.5	---	---	648	644	+4
Cincinnati	68	86	.439	28.5	---	---	559	667	-108
Pittsburgh	64	90	.413	32.5	---	---	689	845	-156
Chicago	62	92	.400	34.5	---	---	614	750	-136

1951 U.S NATIONAL TENNIS CHAMPIONSHIPS

Mens Singles – Frank Sedgman defeated Vic Seixas 6-4, 6-1, 6-1
Womens Singles – Maureen Connolly defeated Shirley Fry 6-3, 1-6, 64
Mens Doubles – Ken McGregor / Frank Sedgman defeated Don Candy / Mervyn Rose 10-8, 6-4, 4-6, 7-5
Womens Doubles – Shirley Fry / Doris Hart defeated Nancy Chaffee / Patricia Todd 6-4, 6-2
Mixed Doubles – Doris Hart / Frank Sedgman defeated Shirley Fry / Mervyn Rose 6-3, 6-2

4

1952

1952 NATIONAL FOOTBALL LEAGUE SEASON
STANDINGS

EAST	W	L	T	WEST	W	L	T
Cleveland	11	1	0	Detroit	10	2	0
Philadelphia	7	4	1	San Francisco	9	3	0
Washington	6	5	1	Los Angeles	8	3	1
Pittsburgh	6	6	0	Chi. Bears	3	8	1
NY Giants	3	9	0	Baltimore	3	9	0
Chi. Cardinals	1	10	1	Green Bay	2	9	1

1952 U.S NATIONAL BADMINTON CHAMPIONOSHIPS
WINNERS

Mens Singles	Womens Singles	Mens Doubles	Womens Doubles	Mixed Doubles
Marten Mendez	Ethel Marshall	Joe Alston Wynn Rogers	Ethel Marshall Beatrice Massman	Wynn Rogers Helen Tibbetts

1952 NBA STANDINGS
DIVISION STANDINGS

Team	W	L	W/L%	GB	PS/G	PA/G	SRS
Eastern Division							
Syracuse Nationals	40	26	.606	---	86.7	82.2	3.94
Boston Celtics	39	27	.591	1.0	91.3	87.2	3.60
New York Knicks	37	29	.561	3.0	85.0	84.2	0.67
Philadelphia Warriors	33	33	.500	7.0	86.5	87.8	-1.08
Baltimore Bullets	20	46	.303	20.0	81.5	89.0	-6.60
Western Division							
Rochester Royals	41	25	.621	---	86.2	82.8	2.92
Minneapolis Lakers	40	26	.606	1.0	85.6	79.5	5.28
Indianapolis Olympians	34	32	.515	7.0	82.9	82.8	0.08
Fort Wayne Pistons	29	37	.439	12.0	78.0	80.1	-1.83
Milwaukee Hawks	17	49	.258	24.0	73.2	81.2	-7.04

AMERICAN HORSE OF THE YEAR
1952 ECLIPSE AWARD

Horse	Trainer	Owner	Age	Gender
Native Dancer	William C. Winfrey	Alfred G. Vanderbilt II	2	C

1952 NHL SEASON
FINAL STANDINGS

National Hockey League	GP	W	L	T	Pts	GF	GA	PIM
Detroit Red Wings	70	36	16	18	90	222	133	645
Montreal Canadiens	70	28	23	19	75	155	148	777
Boston Bruins	70	28	29	13	69	152	172	528
Chicago Blackhawks	70	27	28	15	69	169	175	736
Toronto Maple Leafs	70	27	30	13	67	156	167	812
New York Rangers	70	17	37	16	50	152	211	548

1952 MAJOR LEAGUE BASEBALL SEASON HISTORY

1952 American League Standings

TEAM	W	L	PCT	GB	HOME	ROAD	RS	RA	DIFF
New York	95	59	.617	---	---	---	727	557	+170
Cleveland	93	61	.600	2	---	---	763	606	+157
Chicago	81	73	.519	14	---	---	610	568	+42
Philadelphia	79	75	.510	16	---	---	664	723	-59
Washington	78	76	.497	17	---	---	598	608	-10
Boston	76	78	.494	19	---	---	668	658	+10
St. Louis	64	90	.413	31	---	---	604	733	-129
Detroit	50	104	.321	45	---	---	557	738	-181

1952 National League Standings

TEAM	W	L	PCT	GB	HOME	ROAD	RS	RA	DIFF
Brooklyn	96	57	.619	---	---	---	775	603	+172
New York	92	62	.597	4.5	---	---	722	639	+83
St. Louis	88	66	.571	8.5	---	---	677	630	+47
Philadelphia	87	67	.565	9.5	---	---	657	552	+105
Chicago	77	77	.497	19.5	---	---	628	631	-3
Cincinnati	69	85	.448	27.5	---	---	615	659	-44
Boston	64	89	.413	32	---	---	569	651	-82
Pittsburgh	42	112	.271	54.5	---	---	515	793	-278

1952 U.S NATIONAL TENNIS CHAMPIONSHIPS

Mens Singles – Frank Sedgman defeated Gardnar Mulloy 6-1, 6-2, 6-3
Womens Singles – Maureen Connelly defeated Doris Hart 6-3, 7-5
Mens Doubles – Mervyn Rose / Vic Seixas defeated Ken McGregor / Frank Sedgman 3-6, 10-8, 10-8, 6-8, 8-6
Womens Doubles – Shirley Fry / Doris Hart defeated Louise Brough / Maureen Connelly 10-8, 6-4
Mixed Doubles – Doris Hart / Frank Sedgman defeated Thelma Coyne Long / Lew Hoad 6-3, 7-5

6

1953

1953 NATIONAL FOOTBALL LEAGUE SEASON STANDINGS

EAST	W	L	T	WEST	W	L	T
Cleveland	11	1	0	Detroit	10	2	0
Philadelphia	7	4	1	San Francisco	9	3	0
Washington	6	5	1	Los Angeles	8	3	1
Pittsburgh	6	6	0	Chi. Bears	3	8	1
NY Giants	3	9	0	Baltimore	3	9	0
Chi. Cardinals	1	10	1	Green Bay	2	9	1

1953 U.S NATIONAL BADMINTON CHAMPIONSHIPS WINNERS

Mens Singles	Womens Singles	Mens Doubles	Womens Doubles	Mixed Doubles
David G. Freeman	Ethel Marshall	Joe Alston Wynn Rogers	Judy Devlin Sue Devlin	Joe Alston Lois Alston

1953 NBA STANDINGS DIVISION STANDINGS

Team	W	L	W/L%	GB	PS/G	PA/G	SRS
Eastern Division							
New York Knicks	47	23	.671	---	85.5	80.3	4.39
Syracuse Nationals	47	24	.662	0.5	85.6	81.3	3.62
Boston Celtics	46	25	.648	1.5	88.1	85.8	1.94
Baltimore Bullets	16	54	.229	31.0	84.4	90.9	-5.80
Philadelphia Warriors	12	57	.174	34.5	80.2	87.4	-7.75
Western Division							
Minneapolis Lakers	48	22	.686	---	85.3	79.2	5.54
Rochester Royals	44	26	.629	4.0	86.3	83.5	2.62
Fort Wayne Pistons	36	33	.522	11.5	81.0	81.1	0.17
Indianapolis Olympians	28	43	.394	20.5	74.6	77.4	-2.30
Milwaukee Hawks	27	44	.380	21.5	75.9	77.4	-2.49

AMERICAN HORSE OF THE YEAR
1953 ECLIPSE AWARD

Horse	Trainer	Owner	Age	Gender
Tom Fool	John M. Gaver, Sr.	Greentree Stable	4	C

1953 NHL SEASON
FINAL STANDINGS

National Hockey League	GP	W	L	T	Pts	GF	GA	PIM
Detroit Red Wings	70	37	19	14	88	191	132	814
Montreal Canadiens	70	35	24	11	81	195	141	1064
Toronto Maple Leafs	70	32	24	14	78	152	131	1022
Boston Bruins	70	32	28	10	74	177	181	685
New York Rangers	70	29	31	10	68	161	182	717
Chicago Black Hawks	70	12	51	7	31	133	242	797

1953 MAJOR LEAGUE BASEBALL SEASON HISTORY

1953 American League Standings

TEAM	W	L	PCT	GB	HOME	ROAD	RS	RA	DIFF
New York	99	52	.656	---	---	---	801	547	+254
Cleveland	92	62	.594	8.5	---	---	770	627	+143
Chicago	89	65	.571	11.5	---	---	716	592	+124
Boston	84	69	.549	16	---	---	656	632	+24
Washington	76	76	.500	23.5	---	---	687	614	+73
Detroit	60	94	.380	40.5	---	---	695	923	-228
Philadelphia	59	95	.380	40.5	---	---	632	799	-167
St. Louis	54	100	.351	46.5	---	---	555	778	-223

1953 National League Standings

TEAM	W	L	PCT	GB	HOME	ROAD	RS	RA	DIFF
Brooklyn	105	49	.677	---	---	---	955	689	+266
Milwaukee	92	62	.586	13	---	---	738	589	+149
St. Louis	83	71	.529	22	---	---	768	713	+55
Philadelphia	83	71	.532	22	---	---	716	666	+50
New York	70	84	.452	35	---	---	768	747	+21
Cincinnati	68	86	.439	37	---	---	714	788	-74
Chicago	65	89	.419	40	---	---	633	835	-202
Pittsburgh	50	104	.325	55	---	---	622	887	-265

1953 U.S NATIONAL TENNIS CHAMPIONSHIPS

Mens Singles – Tony Trabert defeated Vic Seixas 6-3, 6-2, 6-3
Womens Singles – Maureen Connelly defeated Doris Hart 6-2, 6-4
Mens Doubles – Rex Hartwig / Mervyn Rose defeated Bill Talbert / Gardnar Mulloy 6-4, 4-6, 6-2, 6-4
Womens Doubles – Shirley Fry / Doris Hart defeated Louise Brough / Margaret Osborne duPont 6-2, 7-9, 9-7
Mixed Doubles – Doris Hart / Vic Seixas defeated Julia Sampson / Rex Hartwig 6-2, 4-6, 6-4

1954

1954 NATIONAL FOOTBALL LEAGUE SEASON STANDINGS

EAST	W	L	T	WEST	W	L	T
Cleveland	9	3	0	Detroit	9	2	1
Philadelphia	7	4	1	Chi. Bears	8	4	0
NY Giants	7	5	0	San Francisco	7	4	1
Pittsburgh	5	7	0	Los Angeles	6	5	1
Washington	3	9	0	Green Bay	4	8	0
Chi. Cardinals	2	10	0	Baltimore	3	9	0

1954 U.S BADMINTON CHAMPIONSHIPS WINNERS

Mens Singles	Womens Singles	Mens Doubles	Womens Doubles	Mixed Doubles
Eddy B. Choong	Judy Devlin	Ooi Teik Hock Ong Poh Lim	Judy Devlin Susan Devlin	Joseph Cameron Alston, Lois Alston

1954 NBA STANDINGS DIVISION STANDINGS

Team	W	L	W/L%	GB	PS/G	PA/G	SRS
Eastern Division							
New York Knicks	44	28	.611	---	79.0	79.1	-0.16
Syracuse Nationals	42	30	.583	2.0	83.5	78.6	4.27
Boston Celtics	42	30	.583	2.0	87.7	85.4	1.97
Philadelphia Warriors	29	43	.403	15.0	78.2	80.4	-1.89
Baltimore Bullets	16	56	.222	28.0	78.3	85.1	-5.98
Western Division							
Minneapolis Lakers	46	26	.639	---	81.7	78.6	2.71
Rochester Royals	44	28	.611	2.0	79.8	77.3	2.24
Fort Wayne Pistons	40	32	.556	6.0	7.77	76.1	1.45
Milwaukee Hawks	21	51	.292	25.0	70.0	75.3	-4.55

AMERICAN HORSE OF THE YEAR
1954 ECLIPSE AWARD

Horse	Trainer	Owner	Age	Gender
Native Dancer	William C. Winfrey	Alfred G. Vanderbilit II	4	C

1954 NHL SEASON
FINAL STANDINGS

National Hockey League	GP	W	L	T	Pts	GF	GA	PIM
Detroit Red Wings	70	42	17	11	95	204	134	827
Montreal Canadiens	70	41	18	11	93	228	157	890
Toronto Maple Leafs	70	24	24	22	70	147	135	990
Boston Bruins	70	23	26	21	67	169	188	863
New York Rangers	70	17	35	18	52	150	210	690
Chicago Black Hawks	70	13	40	17	43	161	235	733

1954 MAJOR LEAGUE BASSEBALL SEASON HISTORY

1954 American League Standings

TEAM	W	L	PCT	GB	HOME	ROAD	RS	RA	DIFF
Cleveland	111	43	.712	---	---	---	746	504	+242
New York	103	51	.665	8	---	---	805	563	+242
Chicago	94	60	.606	17	---	---	711	521	+190
Boston	69	85	.442	42	---	---	700	728	-28
Detroit	68	86	.439	43	---	---	584	664	-80
Washington	66	88	.426	45	---	---	632	680	-48
Baltimore	54	100	.351	57	---	---	483	668	-185
Philadelphia	51	103	.327	60	---	---	542	875	-333

1954 National League Standings

TEAM	W	L	PCT	GB	HOME	ROAD	RS	RA	DIFF
New York	97	57	.630	---	---	---	732	550	+182
Brooklyn	92	62	.597	5	---	---	778	740	+38
Milwaukee	89	65	.578	8	---	---	670	556	+114
Philadelphia	75	79	.487	22	---	---	659	614	+45
Cincinnati	74	80	.481	23	---	---	729	763	-34
St. Louis	72	82	.468	25	---	---	799	790	+9
Chicago	64	90	.416	33	---	---	700	766	-66
Pittsburgh	53	101	.344	44	---	---	557	845	-288

1954 U.S NATIONAL TENNIS CHAMPIONSHIPS

Mens Singles – Vic Seixas defeated Rex Hartwig 3-6, 6-2, 6-4, 6-4
Womens Singles – Doris Hard defeated Louise Brough 6-8, 6-1, 8-6
Mens Doubles – Vic Seixas / Tony Trabert defeated Lew Hoad / Ken Rosewall 3-6, 6-4, 8-6, 6-3
Womens Doubles – Shirley Fry / Doris Hart defeated Louise Brough / Margaret Osborne duPont 6-4, 6-4
Mixed Doubles – Doris Hart / Vic Sexias defeated Margaret Osborne duPont / Ken Rosewall 4-6, 6-1, 6-1

1955

1955 NATIONAL FOOTBALL LEAGUE SEASON STANDINGS

EAST	W	L	T	WEST	W	L	T
Cleveland	9	2	1	Los Angeles	8	3	1
Washington	8	4	0	Chi. Bears	8	4	0
NY Giants	6	5	1	Green Bay	6	6	0
Chi. Cardinals	4	7	1	Baltimore	5	6	1
Philadelphia	4	7	1	San Francisco	4	8	0
Pittsburgh	4	8	0	Detroit	3	9	0

1955 U.S OPEN BADMINTON WINNERS

Mens Singles	Womens Singles	Mens Doubles	Womens Doubles	Mixed Doubles
Joseph C. Alston	Margaret Varner	Joe Alston T. Wynn Rogers	Judy Devlin Susan Devlin	Wynn Rogers Dorothy Hann

1955 NBA STANDINGS DIVISION STANDINGS

Team	W	L	W/L%	GB	PS/G	PA/G	SRS
Eastern Division							
Syracuse Nationals	43	29	.597	---	91.1	89.7	1.23
New York Knicks	38	34	.528	5.0	92.7	92.6	0.11
Boston Celtics	36	36	.500	7.0	101.5	101.5	-0.03
Philadelphia Warriors	33	39	.458	10.0	93.2	93.5	-0.19
Western Division							
Fort Wayne Pistons	43	29	.597	---	92.4	90.0	2.01
Minneapolis Lakers	40	32	.556	3.0	95.6	94.5	0.96
Rochester Royals	29	43	.403	14.0	90.8	92.4	-1.43
Milwaukee Hawks	26	46	.361	17.0	87.4	90.4	-2.66

AMERICAN HORSE OF THE YEAR 1955 ECLIPSE AWARD

Horse	Trainer	Owner	Age	Gender
Nashua	Jim Fitzsimmons	Belair Stud	3	C

11

1955 NHL SEASON
FINAL STANDINGS

National Hockey League	GP	W	L	T	Pts	GF	GA	PIM
Montreal Canadiens	70	45	15	10	100	222	131	977
Detroit Red Wings	70	30	24	16	76	183	148	794
New York Rangers	70	32	28	10	74	204	203	911
Toronto Maple Leafs	70	24	33	13	61	153	181	1051
Boston Bruins	70	23	34	13	59	147	185	929
Chicago Black Hawks	70	19	39	12	50	155	216	826

1955 MAJOR LEAGUE BASEBALL SEASON HISTORY

1995 American League Standings

TEAM	W	L	PCT	GB	HOME	ROAD	RS	RA	DIFF
New York	96	58	.623	---	---	---	762	569	+193
Cleveland	93	61	.604	3	---	---	698	601	+97
Chicago	91	63	.587	5	---	---	725	557	+168
Boston	84	70	.545	12	---	---	755	652	+103
Detroit	79	75	.513	17	---	---	775	658	+117
Kansas City	63	91	.406	33	---	---	638	911	-273
Baltimore	57	97	.365	39	---	---	540	754	-214
Washington	53	101	.344	43	---	---	598	789	-191

1955 National League Standings

TEAM	W	L	PCT	GB	HOME	ROAD	RS	RA	DIFF
Brooklyn	98	55	.636	---	---	---	857	650	+207
Milwaukee	85	69	.552	13.5	---	---	743	668	+75
New York	80	74	.519	18.5	---	---	702	673	+29
Philadelphia	77	77	.500	21.5	---	---	675	666	+9
Cincinnati	75	79	.487	23.5	---	---	761	684	+77
Chicago	72	81	.468	26	---	---	626	713	-87
St. Louis	68	86	.442	30.5	---	---	654	757	-103
Pittsburgh	60	94	.390	38.5	---	---	560	767	-207

1955 U.S NATIONAL TENNIS CHAMPIONSHIPS

Mens Singles – Tony Trabert defeated Ken Rosewall
Womens Singles – Doris Hart defeated Patricia Ward Hales
Mens Doubles – Kosei Kamo / Atsushi Miyagi defeated Gerald Moss / Bill Quillian
Womens Doubles – Louise Brough / Margaret Osborne defeated Shirley Fry / Doris Hart
Mixed Doubles – Doris Hart / Vic Seixas defeated Shirley Fry / Gardnar Mulloy

GAME OF THE YEAR

UCLA WINS 19-17

12

1956

1956 NATIONAL FOOTBALL LEAGUE SEASON STANDINGS

EAST	W	L	T	WEST	W	L	T
NY Giants	8	3	1	Chi. Bears	9	2	1
Chi. Cardinals	7	5	0	Detroit	9	3	0
Washington	6	6	0	San Francisco	5	6	1
Cleveland	5	7	0	Baltimore	5	7	0
Pittsburgh	5	7	0	Green Bay	4	8	0
Philadelphia	3	8	1	Los Angeles	4	8	0

1956 U.S BADMINTON CHAMPIONSHIPS WINNERS

Mens Singles	Womens Singles	Mens Doubles	Womens Doubles	Mixed Doubles
Finn Kobbero	Judy Devlin	Finn Kobbero, Jorgen Hammergaard Hansen	Ethel Marshall Beatrice Massman	Finn Kobbero Judy Devlin

1956 NBA STANDINGS DIVISION STANDINGS

Team	W	L	W/L%	GB	PS/G	PA/G	SRS
Eastern Division							
Philadelphia Warriors	45	27	.625	---	103.1	98.8	3.82
Boston Celtics	39	33	.542	6.0	106.0	105.3	0.72
Syracuse Nationals	35	37	.486	10.0	96.9	96.9	0.17
New York Knicks	35	37	.486	10.0	100.2	100.6	-0.20
Western Division							
Fort Wayne Pistons	37	35	.514	---	94.4	93.7	0.45
Minneapolis Lakers	33	39	.458	4.0	99.3	100.2	-0.92
St. Louis Hawks	33	39	.458	4.0	96.6	98.0	-1.42
Rochester Royals	31	41	.431	6.0	95.8	98.7	-2.61

AMERICAN HORSE OF THE YEAR 1956 ECLIPSE AWARD

Horse	Trainer	Owner	Age	Gender
Swaps	Mesh Tenney	Rex C. Ellsworth	4	C

13

1956 NHL SEASON
FINAL STANDINGS

National Hockey League	GP	W	L	T	Pts	GF	GA	PIM
Detroit Red Wings	70	38	20	12	88	198	157	656
Montreal Canadiens	70	35	23	12	82	210	155	870
Boston Bruins	70	34	24	12	80	195	174	978
New York Rangers	70	26	30	14	66	184	227	870
Toronto Maple Leafs	70	21	34	15	57	174	192	829
Chicago Black Hawks	70	16	39	15	47	169	225	809

1956 MAJOR LEAGUE BASEBALL SEASON HISTORY

1956 American League Standings

TEAM	W	L	PCT	GB	HOME	ROAD	RS	RA	DIFF
New York	97	57	.630	---	---	---	857	631	+226
Cleveland	88	66	.568	9	---	---	712	581	+131
Chicago	85	69	.552	12	---	---	776	634	+142
Boston	84	70	.542	13	---	---	780	751	+29
Detroit	82	72	.529	15	---	---	789	699	+90
Baltimore	69	85	.448	28	---	---	571	705	-134
Washington	59	95	.381	38	---	---	652	924	-272
Kansas City	52	102	.338	45	---	---	619	831	-212

1956 National League Standings

TEAM	W	L	PCT	GB	HOME	ROAD	RS	RA	DIFF
Brooklyn	93	61	.604	---	---	---	720	601	+119
Milwaukee	92	62	.594	1	---	---	709	569	+140
Cincinnati	91	63	.587	2	---	---	775	658	+117
St. Louis	76	78	.487	17	---	---	678	698	-20
Philadelphia	71	83	.461	22	---	---	668	738	-70
New York	67	87	.435	26	---	---	540	650	-110
Pittsburgh	66	88	.420	27	---	---	588	653	-65
Chicago	60	94	.382	33	---	---	597	708	-111

1956 U.S NATIONAL TENNIS CHAMPIONSHIPS

Mens Singles – Ken Rosewall defeated Lew Hoad
Womens Singles – Shirley Fry defeated Althea Gibson
Mens Doubles – Lew Hoad / Ken Rosewall defeated Ham Richardson / Vic Seixas
Womens Doubles – Louise Brough / Margaret Osborne defeated Shirley Fry / Betty Pratt
Mixed Doubles – Margaret Osborne / Ken Rosewall defeated Darlene Hard / Lew Hoad

14

1957

1957 NATIONAL FOOTBALL LEAGUE SEASON STANDINGS

EAST	W	L	T	WEST	W	L	T
Cleveland	9	2	1	Detroit	8	4	0
NY Giants	7	5	0	San Francisco	8	4	0
Pittsburgh	6	6	0	Baltimore	7	5	0
Washington	5	6	1	Los Angeles	6	6	0
Philadelphia	4	8	0	Chi. Bears	5	7	0
Chi. Cardinals	3	9	0	Green Bay	3	9	0

1957 U.S BADMINTON CHAMPIONSHIPS WINNERS

Mens Singles	Womens Singles	Mens Doubles	Womens Doubles	Mixed Doubles
Finn Kobbero	Judy Devlin	Finn Kobbero Jorgen Hammergaard Hansen	Judy Devlin Susan Devlin	Finn Kobbero Judy Devlin

1957 NBA STANDINGS DIVISION STANDINGS

Team	W	L	W/L%	GB	PS/G	PA/G	SRS
Eastern Division							
Boston Celtics	44	28	.611	–	105.5	100.2	4.78
Syracuse Nationals	38	34	.528	6.0	99.7	101.1	-1.03
Philadelphia Warriors	37	35	.514	7.0	100.4	98.9	1.54
New York Knicks	36	36	.500	8.0	100.8	100.9	0.07
Western Division							
St. Louis Hawks	34	38	.472	---	98.5	98.6	-0.27
Minneapolis Lakers	34	38	.472	---	102.3	103.1	-0.89
Fort Wayne Pistons	34	38	.472	---	96.4	98.7	-2.18
Rochester Royals	31	41	.431	3.0	93.4	95.6	-2.08

AMERICAN HORSE OF THE YEAR 1957 ECLIPSE AWARD

Horse	Trainer	Owner	Age	Gender
Bold Ruler	Jim Fitzsimmons	Wheatley Stable	3	C

15

**1957 NHL SEASON
FINAL STANDINGS**

National Hockey League	GP	W	L	T	Pts	GF	GA	PIM
Montreal Canadiens	70	43	17	10	96	250	158	945
New York Rangers	70	32	25	13	77	195	188	781
Detroit Red Wings	70	29	29	12	70	176	207	758
Boston Bruins	70	27	28	15	69	199	194	849
Chicago Black Hawks	70	24	39	7	55	163	202	906
Toronto Maple Leafs	70	21	38	11	53	192	226	861

1957 MAJOR LEAGUE BASEBALL SEASON HISTORY

1957 American League Standings

TEAM	W	L	PCT	GB	HOME	ROAD	RS	RA	DIFF
New York	98	56	.636	---	---	---	723	534	+189
Chicago	90	64	.581	8	---	---	707	566	+141
Boston	82	72	.532	16	---	---	721	668	+53
Detroit	78	76	.506	20	---	---	614	614	0
Baltimore	76	76	.494	21	---	---	597	588	+9
Cleveland	76	77	.497	21.5	---	---	682	722	-40
Kansas City	59	94	.383	38.5	---	---	563	710	-147
Washington	55	99	.357	43	---	---	603	808	-205

1957 National League Standings

TEAM	W	L	PCT	GB	HOME	ROAD	RS	RA	DIFF
Milwaukee	95	59	.613	–	---	---	772	613	+159
St. Louis	87	67	.565	8	–	–	737	666	+71
Brooklyn	84	70	.545	11	---	---	690	591	+99
Cincinnati	80	74	.519	15	---	---	747	781	-34
Philadelphia	77	77	.494	18	---	---	623	656	-33
New York	69	85	.448	26	---	---	643	701	-58
Pittsburgh	62	92	.400	33	---	---	586	696	-110
Chicago	62	92	.397	33	---	---	628	722	-94

1957 U.S NATIONAL TENNIS CHAMPIONSHIPS

Mens Singles – Malcolm Anderson defeated Ashley Cooper
Womens Singles – Althea Gibson defeated Louise Brough
Mens Doubles – Ashley Cooper / Neale Fraser defeated Gardnar Mulloy / Budge Patty
Womens Doubles – Louise Brough / Margaret Osborne defeated Althea Gibson / Darlene Hard
Mixed Doubles – Althea Gibson / Kurt Nielsen defeated Darlene Hard / Bob Howe

1958

1958 NATIONAL FOOTBALL LEAGUE SEASON STANDINGS

EAST	W	L	T	WEST	W	L	T
NY Giants	9	3	0	Baltimore	9	3	0
Cleveland	9	3	0	Chi. Bears	8	4	0
Pittsburgh	7	4	1	Los Angeles	8	4	0
Washington	4	7	1	San Francisco	6	6	0
Chi. Cardinals	2	9	1	Chi. Detroit	4	7	1
Philadelphia	2	9	1	Green Bay	1	10	1

1958 U.S BADMINTON CHAMPIONSHIPS WINNERS

Mens Singles	Womens Singles	Mens Doubles	Womens Doubles	Mixed Doubles
Jim Poole	Judy Devlin	Finn Kobbero Jorgen Hammergaard Hansen	Judy Devlin Susan Devlin	Finn Kobbero Judy Devlin

1958 NBA STANDINGS DIVISION STANDINGS

Team	W	L	W/L%	GB	PS/G	PA/G	SRS
Eastern Division							
Boston Celtics	49	23	.681	–	109.9	104.4	5.02
Syracuse Nationals	41	31	.569	8.0	107.2	105.1	2.18
Philadelphia Warriors	37	35	.514	12.0	104.3	104.4	0.21
New York Knicks	35	37	.486	14.0	112.1	110.8	1.35
Western Division							
St. Louis Hawks	41	31	.569	---	107.5	106.2	0.82
Detroit Pistons	33	39	.458	8.0	105.3	107.7	-2.32
Cincinnati Royals	33	39	.458	8.0	101.7	103.1	-1.47
Minneapolis Lakers	19	53	.264	22.0	105.1	111.5	-5.78

AMERICAN HORSE OF THE YEAR 1958 ECLIPSE AWARD

Horse	Trainer	Owner	Age	Gender
Roundtable	William Molter	Kerr Stable	4	C

1958 NHL SEASON
FINAL STANDINGS

National Hockey League	GP	W	L	T	Pts	GF	GA	PIM
Montreal Canadiens	70	39	18	13	91	258	158	760
Boston Bruins	70	32	29	9	73	205	215	838
Chicago Black Hawks	70	28	29	13	69	197	208	921
Toronto Maple Leafs	70	27	32	11	65	189	201	846
New York Rangers	70	26	32	12	64	201	217	860
Detroit Red Wings	70	25	37	8	58	167	218	613

1958 MAJOR LEAGUE BASEBALL SEASON HISTORY

1958 American League Standings

TEAM	W	L	PCT	GB	HOME	ROAD	RS	RA	DIFF
New York	92	62	.594	---	---	---	759	577	+182
Chicago	82	72	.529	10	---	---	634	615	+19
Boston	79	75	.510	13	---	---	697	691	+6
Cleveland	77	76	.503	14.5	---	---	694	635	+59
Detroit	77	77	.500	15	---	---	659	606	+53
Baltimore	74	79	.481	17.5	---	---	521	575	-54
Kansas City	73	81	.468	19	---	---	642	713	-71
Washington	61	93	.391	31	---	---	553	747	-194

1958 National League Standings

TEAM	W	L	PCT	GB	HOME	ROAD	RS	RA	DIFF
Milwaukee	92	62	.597	–	---	---	675	541	+134
Pittsburgh	84	70	.545	8	–	–	662	607	+55
San Francisco	80	74	.519	12	---	---	727	698	+29
Cincinnati	76	78	.494	16	---	---	695	621	+74
St. Louis	72	82	.468	20	---	---	619	704	-85
Chicago	72	82	.468	20	---	---	709	725	-16
Los Angeles	71	83	.461	21	---	---	668	761	-93
Philadelphia	69	85	.448	23	---	---	664	762	-98

1958 U.S NATIONAL TENNIS CHAMPIONSHIPS

Mens Singles – Cooper defeated Malcolm Anderson
Womens Singles – Althea Gibson defeated Darlene Hard
Mens Doubles – Alex Olmedo / Ham Richardson defeated Sam Giammalva / Barry MacKay
Womens Doubles – Jeanne Arth / Darlene Hard defeated Althea Gibson / Maria Bueno
Mixed Doubles – Margret Osborne / Neale Fraser defeated Maria Bueno / Alex Olmedo

18

1959

NATIONAL FOOTBALL LEAGUE SEASON STANDINGS

EAST	W	L	T	WEST	W	L	T
NY Giants	10	2	0	Baltimore	9	3	0
Cleveland	7	5	0	Chi. Bears	8	4	0
Philadelphia	7	5	1	Green Bay	7	5	0
Pittsburgh	6	5	1	San Francisco	7	5	0
Washington	3	9	1	Detroit	3	8	0
Chi. Cardinals	2	10	1	Los Angeles	2	10	1

U.S BADMINTON CHAMPIONSHIPS WINNERS

Mens Singles	Womens Singles	Mens Doubles	Womens Doubles	Mixed Doubles
Tan Joe Hok	Judy Devlin	Teh Kew San Kim Say Hup	Judy Devlin Susan Devlin	Michael Roche Judy Devlin

NBA STANDINGS DIVISION STANDINGS

Team	W	L	W/L%	GB	PS/G	PA/G	SRS
Eastern Division							
Boston Celtics	52	20	.722	–	116.4	109.9	5.84
New York Knicks	40	32	.556	12.0	110.3	110.1	0.49
Syracuse Nationals	35	37	.486	17.0	113.1	109.1	3.74
Philadelphia Warriors	32	40	.444	20.0	103.3	106.3	-2.29
Western Division							
St. Louis Hawks	49	23	.681	---	108.8	105.1	5.84
Minneapolis Lakers	33	39	.458	16.0	106,0	107.3	0.49
Detroit Pistons	28	44	.389	21.0	105.1	106.3	3.74
Cincinnati Royals	19	53	.264	30.0	103.1	109.1	.7.89

AMERICAN HORSE OF THE YEAR ECLIPSE AWARD

Horse	Trainer	Owner	Age	Gender
Sword Dancer	J. Elliot Burch	Brooke Meade Stable	3	C

NHL SEASON
FINAL STANDINGS

National Hockey League	GP	W	L	T	Pts	GF	GA	PIM
Montreal Canadiens	70	40	18	12	92	255	178	756
Toronto Maple Leafs	70	35	26	9	79	199	195	859
Chicago Black Hawks	70	28	29	13	69	191	180	970
Detroit Red Wings	70	26	29	15	67	186	197	528
Boston Bruins	70	28	34	8	64	220	241	932
New York Rangers	70	17	38	15	49	187	247	850

MAJOR LEAGUE BASEBALL SEASON HISTORY
American League Standings

TEAM	W	L	PCT	GB	HOME	ROAD	RS	RA	DIFF
Chicago	94	60	.603	---	---	---	669	588	+81
Cleveland	89	65	.578	5	---	---	745	646	+99
New York	79	85	.510	15	---	---	687	647	+40
Detroit	76	78	.494	18	---	---	713	732	-19
Boston	75	79	.487	19	---	---	726	696	+30
Baltimore	74	80	.477	20	---	---	551	621	-70
Kansas City	66	88	.429	28	---	---	881	760	-79
Washington	63	91	.409	31	---	---	619	701	-82

National League Standings

TEAM	W	L	PCT	GB	HOME	ROAD	RS	RA	DIFF
Los Angeles	88	68	.564	---	---	---	705	670	+35
Milwaukee	86	70	.548	2	---	---	724	623	+101
San Francisco	83	71	.539	4	---	---	705	613	+92
Pittsburgh	78	76	.503	9	---	---	651	680	-29
Cincinnati	74	80	.481	13	---	---	764	738	+26
Chicago	74	80	.477	13	---	---	673	688	-15
St. Louis	71	83	.461	16	---	---	641	725	-84
Philadelphia	64	90	.413	23	---	---	599	725	-126

U.S NATIONAL TENNIS CHAMPIONSHIPS

Mens Singles – Neale Fraser defeated Alex Olmedo
Womens Singles – Maria Bueno defeated Christine Truman
Mens Doubles – Neale Fraser / Roy Emerson defeated Alex Olmedo / Earl Buchholz
Womens Doubles – Jeanne Arth / Darlene Hard defeated Althea Gibson / Sally Moore
Mixed Doubles – Margaret Osborne / Neale Fraser defeated Janet Hopps / Bob Mark

1960

NATIONAL FOOTBALL LEAGUE SEASON STANDINGS

EAST	W	L	T	WEST	W	L	T
Philadelphia	10	2	0	Green Bay	8	4	0
Cleveland	8	3	0	Detroit	7	5	0
NY Giants	6	4	1	San Francisco	7	5	0
St. Louis	6	5	1	Baltimore	6	6	1
Pittsburgh	5	6	1	Chicago	5	6	1
Washington	1	9	1	Los Angeles	4	7	1

U.S BADMINTON CHAMPIONSHIPS WINNERS

Mens Singles	Womens Singles	Mens Doubles	Womens Doubles	Mixed Doubles
Tan Joe Hok	Judy Devlin	Finn Kobbero, Charoen Wattanasin	Judy Devlin Susan Devlin	Finn Kobbero, Margaret Varner

NBA STANDINGS DIVISION STANDINGS

Team	W	L	W/L%	GB	PS/G	PA/G	SRS
Eastern Division							
Boston Celtics	59	16	.787	–	124.5	116.2	7.62
Philadelphia Warriors	49	26	.653	10.0	118.6	116.0	2.77
Syracuse Nationals	45	30	.600	14.0	118.9	116.3	2.77
New York Knick	27	48	.360	32.0	117.3	119.6	-1.43
Western Division							
St. Louis Hawks	46	29	.613	---	113.4	110.7	1.77
Detroit Pistons	30	45	.400	16.0	111.6	115.0	-3.45
Minneapolis Lakers	25	50	.333	21.0	107.3	111.5	-4.14
Cincinnati Royals	19	56	.253	27.0	111.1	117.4	-5.92

AMERICAN HORSE OF THE YEAR ECLIPSE AWARD

Horse	Trainer	Owner	Age	Gender
Kelso	Carl Hanford	Bohemia Stable	3	G

21

NHL SEASON
FINAL STANDINGS

National Hockey League	GP	W	L	T	Pts	GF	GA	PIM
Montreal Canadiens	70	41	19	10	92	254	188	811
Toronto Maple Leafs	70	39	19	12	90	234	176	844
Chicago Black Hawks	70	29	24	17	75	198	180	1072
Detroit Red Wings	70	25	29	16	66	195	215	655
New York Rangers	70	22	38	10	54	204	248	591
Boston Bruins	70	15	42	13	43	176	254	810

MAJOR LEAGUE BASEBALL SEASON HISTORY
American League Standings

TEAM	W	L	PCT	GB	HOME	ROAD	RS	RA	DIFF
New York	97	57	.626	---	---	---	746	627	+119
Baltimore	89	65	.578	8	---	---	682	606	+76
Chicago	87	67	.565	10	---	---	741	617	+124
Cleveland	76	78	.494	21	---	---	667	693	-26
Washington	73	81	.474	24	---	---	672	696	-24
Detroit	71	83	.461	26	---	---	633	644	-11
Boston	65	89	.422	32	---	---	658	775	-117
Kansas City	58	96	.374	39	---	---	615	756	-141

National League Standings

TEAM	W	L	PCT	GB	HOME	ROAD	RS	RA	DIFF
Pittsburgh	95	59	.613	---	---	—	734	593	+141
Milwaukee	88	66	.571	7	---	---	724	658	+66
St. Louis	86	68	.555	9	---	---	639	616	+23
Los Angeles	82	72	.532	13	---	—	662	593	+69
San Francisco	79	75	.506	16	---	---	671	631	+40
Cincinnati	67	87	.435	28	---	---	640	692	-52
Chicago	60	94	.385	35	---	---	634	776	-142
Philadelphia	59	95	.383	36	---	---	546	691	-145

U.S NATIONAL TENNIS CHAMPIONSHIPS

Mens Singles – Neale Fraser defeated Rod Laver
Womens Singles – Darlene Hard defeated Maria Bueno
Mens Doubles – Neale Fraser / Roy Emerson defeated Rod Laver / Bob Mark
Womens Doubles – Maria Bueno / Darlene Hard defeated Ann Haydono Jones / Deidre Catt
Mixed Doubles – Margaret Osborn / Neale Fraser defeated Maria Bueno / Antonio Palafox

1961

NATIONAL FOOTBALL LEAGUE SEASON STANDINGS

EAST	W	L	T	WEST	W	L	T
NY Giants	10	3	1	Green Bay	11	3	0
Philadelphia	10	4	0	Detroit	8	5	1
Cleveland	8	5	1	Baltimore	8	6	0
St. Louis	7	7	0	Chicago	8	6	0
Pittsburgh	6	8	0	San Francisco	7	6	1
Dallas	4	9	1	Los Angeles	4	10	0

U.S BADMINTON CHAMPIONSHIPS WINNERS

Mens Singles	Womens Singles	Mens Doubles	Womens Doubles	Mixed Doubles
Jim Poole	Judy Devlin	Joe Alston Wynn Rogers	Judy Devlin Susan Devlin	Wynn Rogers Judy Devlin

NBA STANDINGS DIVISION STANDINGS

Team	W	L	W/L%	GB	PS/G	PA/G	SRS
Eastern Division							
Boston Celtics	57	22	.722	–	119.7	114.1	4.94
Philadelphia Warriors	46	33	.582	11.0	121.0	120.1	0.89
Syracuse Nationals	38	41	.481	19.0	121.3	119.2	1.93
New York Knicks	21	58	.266	36.0	113.7	120.1	-5.43
Western Division							
St. Louis Hawks	51	28	.646	---	118.8	115.2	2.99
Los Angeles Lakers	36	43	.456	15.0	114.0	114.1	-0.11
Detroit Pistons	34	45	.430	17.0	118.6	121.0	-2.11
Cincinnati Royals	33	46	.418	18.0	117.9	121.3	-3.04

AMERICAN HORSE OF THE YEAR ECLIPSE AWARD

Horse	Trainer	Owner	Age	Gender
Kelso	Carl Hanford	Bohemia Stable	4	G

23

NHL SEASON
FINAL STANDINGS

National Hockey League	GP	W	L	T	Pts	GF	GA	PIM
Montreal Canadiens	70	41	19	10	92	254	188	811
Toronto Maple Leafs	70	39	19	12	90	234	176	844
Chicago Black Hawks	70	29	24	17	75	198	180	1072
Detroit Red Wings	70	25	29	16	66	195	215	655
New York Rangers	70	22	38	10	54	204	248	591
Boston Bruins	70	15	42	13	43	176	254	810

MAJOR LEAGUE BASEBALL SEASON HISTORY
American League Standings

TEAM	W	L	PCT	GB	HOME	ROAD	RS	RA	DIFF
New York	97	57	.626	---	---	---	746	627	+119
Baltimore	89	65	.578	8	---	---	682	606	+76
Chicago	87	67	.565	10	---	---	741	617	+124
Cleveland	76	78	.494	21	---	---	667	693	-26
Washington	73	81	.474	24	---	---	672	696	-24
Detroit	71	83	.461	26	---	---	633	644	-11
Boston	65	89	.422	32	---	---	658	756	-141
Kansas City	58	96	.374	39	---	---	615	756	-141

National League Standings

TEAM	W	L	PCT	GB	HOME	ROAD	RS	RA	DIFF
Pittsburgh	95	59	.613	---	---	---	734	593	+141
Milwaukee	88	66	.571	7	---	---	724	658	+66
St. Louis	86	68	.555	9	---	---	639	616	+23
Los Angeles	82	72	.532	13	---	---	662	593	+69
San Francisco	79	75	.506	16	---	---	671	631	+40
Cincinnati	67	87	.435	28	---	---	640	692	-52
Chicago	60	94	.385	35	---	---	634	776	-142
Philadelphia	59	95	.383	36	---	---	546	691	-145

U.S NATIONAL TENNIS CHAMPIONSHIPS

Mens Singles – Roy Emerson defeated Rod Laver
Womens Singles – Darlene Hard defeated Ann Haydon Jones
Mens Doubles – Chuck McKinley / Dennis Ralston defeated Rafael Osuna / Antonio Palafox
Womens Doubles – Darlene Hard / Lesley Turner defeated Edda Buding / Yola Ramirez
Mixed Doubles – Margaret Smith / Bob Mark defeated Darlene Hard / Dennis Ralston

1962

NATIONAL FOOTBALL LEAGUE SEASON STANDINGS

EAST	W	L	T	WEST	W	L	T
NY Giants	12	2	0	Green Bay	13	1	0
Pittsburgh	9	5	0	Detroit	11	3	0
Cleveland	7	6	1	Chicago	9	5	0
Washington	5	7	2	Baltimore	7	7	0
St. Louis	4	9	1	Minnesota	2	11	1
Philadelphia	3	10	1	Los Angeles	1	12	1

U.S BADMINTON CHAMPIONSHIPS WINNERS

Mens Singles	Womens Singles	Mens Doubles	Womens Doubles	Mixed Doubles
Ferry Sonneville	Judy Devlin	Joe Alston Wynn Rogers	Judy Hashman Patsy Stephens	Wynn Rogers Judy Hashman

NBA STANDINGS DIVISION STANDINGS

Team	W	L	W/L%	GB	PS/G	PA/G	SRS
Eastern Division							
Boston Celtics	60	20	.750	–	121.1	111.9	8.25
Philadelphia Warriors	49	31	.613	11.0	125.4	122.7	2.63
Syracuse Nationals	41	39	.513	19.0	120.7	118.4	2.24
New York Knicks	29	51	.363	31.0	114.8	119.7	-3.98
Western Division							
Los Angeles Lakers	54	26	.675	---	118.5	116.3	1.80
Cincinnati Royals	43	37	.538	11.0	123.1	121.3	1.28
St. Louis Hawks	29	51	.363	25.0	118.9	122.1	-2.96
Chicago Packers	18	62	.225	36.0	110.9	119.4	-7.54

AMERICAN HORSE OF THE YEAR ECLIPSE AWARD

Horse	Trainer	Owner	Age	Gender
Kelso	Carl Hanford	Bohemia Stable	5	G

NHL SEASON
FINAL STANDINGS

National Hockey League	GP	W	L	T	Pts	GF	GA	PIM
Toronto Maple Leafs	70	35	23	12	82	221	180	816
Chicago Black Hawks	70	32	21	17	81	194	178	906
Montreal Canadiens	70	28	19	23	79	225	183	751
Detroit Red Wings	70	32	25	13	77	200	194	964
New York Rangers	70	22	36	12	56	211	233	657
Boston Bruins	70	14	39	17	45	198	281	636

MAJOR LEAGUE BASEBALL SEASON HISTORY
American League Standings

TEAM	W	L	PCT	GB	HOME	ROAD	RS	RA	DIFF
New York	96	66	.593	---	---	---	817	680	_137
Minnesota	91	71	.558	5	---	---	798	713	+85
Los Angeles	86	76	.531	10	---	---	718	706	+12
Detroit	85	76	.528	10.5	---	—	758	692	+66
Chicago	85	77	.525	11	---	---	707	658	+49
Cleveland	80	82	.494	16	---	---	682	745	-63
Baltimore	77	85	.475	19	---	---	652	680	-28
Boston	76	84	.475	19	---	---	707	756	-49
Kansas City	72	90	.444	24	---	---	745	837	-92
Washington	60	101	.370	35.5	---	---	599	716	-117

National League Standings

TEAM	W	L	PCT	GB	HOME	ROAD	RS	RA	DIFF
San Francisco	103	62	.624	---	---	---	878	690	+188
Los Angeles	102	63	.618	1	---	---	842	697	+145
Cincinnati	98	64	.605	3.5	---	---	802	685	+117
Pittsburgh	93	68	.578	8	---	---	706	626	+80
Milwaukee	86	76	.531	15.5	---	---	730	665	+65
St. Louis	84	78	.515	17.5	---	---	774	664	+110
Philadelphia	81	80	.503	20	---	---	705	759	-54
Houston	64	96	.395	36.5	---	---	592	717	-125
Chicago	59	103	.364	42.5	---	---	632	827	-195
New York	40	120	.248	60.5	---	---	617	948	-331

U.S NATIONAL TENNIS CHAMPIONSHIPS

Mens Singles – Rod Laver defeated Roy Emerson
Womens Singles – Margaret Smith defeated Darlene Hard
Mens Doubles – Rafael Osuna / Antonio Palafox defeated Chuck McKinley / Dennis Ralston
Womens Doubles – Darlene Hard / Maria Bueno defeated Karen Hantze Susman / Billie Jean Moffitt
Mixed Doubles – Margaret Smith / Fred Stolle defeated Lesley Turner / Frank Froehling

1963

NATIONAL FOOTBALL LEAGUE SEASON
STANDINGS

EAST	W	L	T	WEST	W	L	T
NY Giants	11	3	0	Chicago	11	1	2
Cleveland	10	4	0	Green Bay	11	2	1
St. Louis	9	5	0	Baltimore	8	6	0
Pittsburgh	7	4	3	Detroit	5	8	1
Dallas	4	10	0	Minnesota	5	8	1
Washington	3	11	0	Los Angeles	5	9	0
Philadelphia	2	10	2	San Francisco	2	12	0

U.S BADMINTON CHAMPIONSHIPS
WINNERS

Mens Singles	Womens Singles	Mens Doubles	Womens Doubles	Mixed Doubles
Erland Kops	Judy Devlin	Erland Kops Bob McCoig	Judy Hashman Susan Peard	Sangob Rattanusorn Margaret Barrand

NBA STANDINGS
DIVISION STANDINGS

Team	W	L	W/L%	GB	PS/G	PA/G	SRS
Eastern Division							
Boston Celtics	58	22	.725	–	118.8	111.6	6.38
Syracuse Nationals	48	32	.600	10.0	121.6	117.8	3.40
Cincinnati Royals	42	38	.525	16.0	119.1	117.8	1.24
New York Knicks	21	59	.263	37.0	110.5	117.7	-6.20
Western Division							
Los Angeles Lakers	53	27	.663	---	115.5	112.4	2.67
St. Louis Hawks	48	32	.600	5.0	109.6	107.8	1.38
Detroit Pistons	34	46	.425	19.0	113.9	117.6	-3.38
San Francisco Warriors	31	49	.388	22.0	118.5	120.6	-1.86
Chicago Zephyrs	25	55	.313	28.0	109.9	114.0	-3.63

AMERICAN HORSE OF THE YEAR
ECLIPSE AWARD

Horse	Trainer	Owner	Age	Gender
Kelso	Carl Hanford	Bohemia Stable	6	G

27

NHL SEASON
FINAL STANDINGS

National Hockey League	GP	W	L	T	Pts	GF	GA	PIM
Montreal Canadiens	70	36	21	13	85	209	167	982
Chicago Black Hawks	70	36	22	12	84	218	169	1116
Toronto Maple Leafs	70	33	25	12	78	192	172	928
Detroit Red Wings	70	30	29	11	71	191	204	771
New York Rangers	70	22	38	10	54	186	242	715
Boston Bruins	17	18	40	12	48	170	212	858

MAJOR LEAGUE BASEBALL SEASON HISTORY
American League Standings

TEAM	W	L	PCT	GB	HOME	ROAD	RS	RA	DIFF
New York	104	57	.646	---	---	---	714	547	+167
Chicago	94	68	.580	10.5	---	---	683	544	+139
Minnesota	91	70	.565	13	---	---	767	602	+165
Baltimore	86	76	.531	18.5	---	---	644	621	+23
Detroit	79	83	.488	25.5	---	---	700	703	-3
Cleveland	79	83	.488	25.5	---	---	635	702	-67
Boston	76	85	.472	28	---	---	666	704	-38
Kansas City	73	89	.451	31.5	---	---	615	704	-89
Los Angeles	70	91	.435	34	---	---	597	660	-63
Washington	56	106	.346	48.5	---	---	578	812	-234

National League Standings

TEAM	W	L	PCT	GB	HOME	ROAD	RS	RA	DIFF
Los Angeles	99	63	.607	---	---	---	640	550	+90
St. Louis	93	69	.574	6	---	---	747	628	+119
San Francisco	88	74	.543	11	—	---	725	641	+84
Philadelphia	87	75	.537	12	---	---	642	578	+64
Cincinnati	86	76	.531	13	---	---	648	594	+54
Milwaukee	84	78	.515	15	---	---	677	603	+74
Chicago	82	80	.506	17	---	---	570	578	-8
Pittsburgh	74	88	.457	25	---	---	567	595	-28
Houston	66	96	.407	33	---	---	464	640	-176
New York	51	111	.315	48	---	---	501	774	-273

U.S NATIONAL TENNIS CHAMPIONSHIPS

Mens Singles – Rafael Osuna defeated Frank Froehling
Womens Singles – Maria Bueno defeated Margaret Smith
Mens Doubles – Chuck McKinley / Dennis Ralston defeated Rafael Osuna / Antonio Palafox
Womens Doubles – Robyn Ebbern / Margaret Smith defeated Darlene Hard / Maria Bueno
Mixed Doubles – Margaret Smith / Ken Fletcher defeated Judy Tegart / Ed Rubinoff

1964

NATIONAL FOOTBALL LEAGUE SEASON STANDINGS

EAST	W	L	T	WEST	W	L	T
Cleveland	10	3	1	Baltimore	12	2	0
St. Louis	9	3	2	Green Bay	8	5	1
Philadelphia	6	8	0	Minnesota	8	5	1
Washington	6	8	0	Detroit	7	5	2
Dallas	5	8	1	Los Angeles	5	7	2
Pittsburgh	5	9	0	Chicago	5	9	0
NY Giants	2	10	2	San Francisco	4	10	0

U.S BADMINTON CHAMPIONSHIPS WINNERS

Mens Singles	Womens Singles	Mens Doubles	Womens Doubles	Mixed Doubles
Channarong Ratanaseangsuang	Dorothy O'Niel	Joe Alston Wynn Rogers	Tyna Barinaga Caroline Jensen	Channarong Ratanaseangsuang, Margaret Barrand

NBA STANDINGS DIVISION STANDINGS

Team	W	L	W/L%	GB	PS/G	PA/G	SRS
Eastern Division							
Boston Celtics	59	21	.738	–	113.0	105.1	6.93
Cincinnati Royals	55	25	.688	4.0	114.7	109.7	4.43
Philadelphia 76ers	34	46	.425	25.0	112.2	116.5	-3.75
New York Knicks	22	58	.275	37.0	112.2	119.0	-5.91
Western Division							
San Francisco Warriors	48	32	.600	---	107.7	102.6	4.41
St. Louis Hawks	46	34	.575	2.0	110.0	108.4	1.39
Los Angeles Lakers	42	38	.525	6.0	109.7	108.7	0.87
Baltimore Bullets	31	49	.388	17.0	111.9	113.6	-1.59

AMERICAN HORSE OF THE YEAR ECLIPSE AWARD

Horse	Trainer	Owner	Age	Gender
Kelso	Carl Hanford	Bohemia Stable	7	G

NHL SEASON
FINAL STANDINGS

National Hockey League	GP	W	L	T	Pts	GF	GA	PIM
Detroit Red Wings	70	40	23	7	87	224	175	1121
Montreal Canadiens	70	36	23	11	83	211	185	1033
Chicago Black Hawks	70	34	28	8	76	224	176	1051
Toronto Maple Leafs	70	30	26	14	74	204	173	1068
New York Rangers	70	20	38	12	52	179	246	760
Boston Bruins	70	21	43	6	48	166	253	946

MAJOR LEAGUE BASEBALL SEASON HISTORY
American League Standings

TEAM	W	L	PCT	GB	HOME	ROAD	RS	RA	DIFF
New York	99	63	.604	---	---	---	730	577	+153
Chicago	98	64	.605	1	---	---	642	501	+141
Baltimore	97	65	.595	2	---	---	679	567	+112
Detroit	85	77	.521	14	---	---	699	678	+21
Los Angeles	82	80	.506	17	---	---	544	551	-7
Minnesota	79	83	.485	20	---	---	737	678	+59
Cleveland	79	83	.482	20	---	---	689	693	-4
Boston	72	90	.444	27	---	---	688	793	-105
Washington	62	100	.383	37	---	---	578	733	-155
Kansas City	57	105	.350	42	---	---	621	836	-215

National League Standings

TEAM	W	L	PCT	GB	HOME	ROAD	RS	RA	DIFF
St. Louis	93	69	.574	---	---	---	715	652	+63
Philadelphia	92	70	.568	1	---	---	693	632	+61
Cincinnati	92	70	.564	1	---	---	660	566	+94
San Francisco	90	72	.556	3	---	---	656	587	+69
Milwaukee	88	74	.543	5	---	---	803	744	+59
Pittsburgh	80	82	.494	13	---	---	663	636	+27
Los Angeles	80	82	.488	13	---	---	614	572	+42
Chicago	76	86	.469	17	---	---	649	724	-75
Houston	66	96	.407	27	---	---	495	628	-133
New York	53	109	.325	40	---	---	569	776	-207

U.S NATIONAL TENNIS CHAMPIONSHIPS

Mens Singles – Roy Emerson defeated Fred Stolle
Womens Singles – Maria Bueno defeated Carole Caldwell Graebner
Mens Doubles – Chuck McKinley / Dennis Ralsto defeated Graham Stilwell / Mike Sangster
Womens Doubles – Billie Jean Moffitt / Karen Susman defeated Margaret Smith / Lesley Turner
Mixed Doubles – Margaret Smith / John Newcombe defeated Judy Tegart / Ed Rubinoff

1965

NATIONAL FOOTBALL LEAGUE SEASON
STANDINGS

EAST	W	L	T	WEST	W	L	T
Cleveland	11	3	0	Green Bay	10	3	1
Dallas	7	7	0	Baltimore	10	3	1
NY Giants	7	7	0	Chicago	9	5	0
Washington	6	8	0	San Francisco	7	6	1
Philadelphia	5	9	0	Minnesota	7	7	0
St. Louis	5	9	0	Detroit	6	7	1
Pittsburgh	2	12	0	Los Angeles	4	10	0

U.S BADMINTON CHAMPIONSHIPS
WINNERS

Mens Singles	Womens Singles	Mens Doubles	Womens Doubles	Mixed Doubles
Erland Kops	Judy Devlin	Bob McCoig Tony Jordan	Margaret Barrand Jennifer Pritchard	Bob McCoig Margaret Barrand

NBA STANDINGS
DIVISION STANDINGS

Team	W	L	W/L%	GB	PS/G	PA/G	SRS
Eastern Division							
Boston Celtics	62	18	.775	–	112.8	104.4	7.46
Cincinnati Royals	48	32	.600	14.0	114.2	111.9	2.04
Philadelphia 76ers	40	40	.500	22.0	112.5	112.7	-0.13
New York Knicks	31	49	.388	31.0	107.4	111.1	-3.26
Western Division							
Los Angeles Laker	49	31	.613	------	111.9	109.9	1.70
St. Louis Hawks	45	35	.563	4.0	108.8	105.8	2.68
Baltimore Bullets	37	43	.463	12.0	113.6	115.8	-1.97
Detroit Pistons	31	49	.388	18.0	108.5	111.9	-3.03
San Francisco Warriors	17	63	.213	32.0	105.8	112.0	-5.49

AMERICAN HORSE OF THE YEAR
ECLIPSE AWARD

Horse	Trainer	Owner	Age	Gender
Moccasin	Harry Trotsek	Claiborne Farm	2	F
Roman Brother	Burley Parke	Harbor View Farm	4	G

NHL SEASON
FINAL STANDINGS

National Hockey League	GP	W	L	T	Pts	GF	GA	PIM
Montreal Canadiens	70	41	21	8	90	239	173	884
Chicago Black Hawks	70	37	25	8	82	240	187	815
Toronto Maple Leafs	70	34	25	11	79	208	187	811
Detroit Red Wings	70	31	27	12	74	221	194	804
Boston Bruins	70	21	43	6	48	174	275	787
New York Rangers	70	18	41	11	47	195	261	894

MAJOR LEAGUE BASEBALL SEASON HISTORY
American League Standings

TEAM	W	L	PCT	GB	HOME	ROAD	RS	RA	DIFF
Minnesota	102	60	.630	---	---	---	774	600	+174
Chicago	95	67	,586	7	---	---	647	555	+92
Baltimore	94	68	.580	8	---	---	641	578	+63
Detroit	89	73	.549	13	---	---	680	602	+78
Cleveland	87	75	.537	15	---	---	663	613	+50
New York	77	85	.475	25	---	---	611	604	+7
California	75	87	.463	27	---	---	527	569	-42
Washington	70	92	.432	32	---	---	591	721	-130
Boston	62	100	.383	40	---	---	669	791	-122
Kansas City	59	103	.364	43	---	---	585	755	-170

National League Standings

TEAM	W	L	PCT	GB	HOME	ROAD	RS	RA	DIFF
Los Angeles	97	65	.599	---	---	---	608	521	+87
San Francisco	95	67	.583	2	---	---	682	593	+89
Pittsburgh	90	72	.552	7	---	---	675	580	+95
Cincinnati	89	73	.549	8	---	---	825	704	+121
Milwaukee	86	76	.531	11	---	---	708	633	+75
Philadelphia	85	76	.525	11.5	---	---	654	667	-13
St. Louis	80	81	.494	16.5	---	---	707	674	+33
Chicago	72	90	.439	25	---	---	635	723	-88
Houston	65	97	.401	32	---	---	569	711	-142
New York	50	112	.305	47	---	---	495	752	-257

U.S NATIONAL TENNIS CHAMPIONSHIPS

Mens Singles – Manuel Santana defeated Cliff Drysdale
Womens Singles – Margaret Smith defeated Billie Jean Moffitt
Mens Doubles – Roy Emerson / Fred Stolle defeated Frank Froehling / Charles Pasarell
Womens Doubles – Carole Graebner / Nancy Richey defeated Billie Jean Moffitt / Karen Susman
Mixed Doubles – Margaret Smith / Fred Stolle defeated Judy Tegart / Frank Froehling

1966

NATIONAL FOOTBALL LEAGUE SEASON
STANDINGS

EAST	W	L	T	WEST	W	L	T
Dallas	10	3	1	Green Bay	12	2	0
Cleveland	9	5	0	Baltimore	9	5	0
Philadelphia	9	5	0	Los Angeles	8	6	0
St. Louis	8	5	1	San Francisco	6	6	2
Washington	7	7	0	Chicago	5	7	2
Pittsburgh	5	8	1	Detroit	4	9	1
Atlanta	3	11	0	Minnesota	4	9	1

U.S BADMINTON CHAMPIONSHIPS
WINNERS

Mens Singles	Womens Singles	Mens Doubles	Womens Doubles	Mixed Doubles
Tan Aik Huang	Judy Devlin	Ng Boon Bee, Tan Yee Khan	Judy Hashman Susan Peard	Wayne MacDonnell Tyna Barinaga

NBA STANDINGS
DIVISION STANDINGS

Team	W	L	W/L%	GB	PS/G	PA/G	SRS
Eastern Division							
Philadelphia 76ers	55	25	.688	–	117.3	112.7	4.16
Boston Celtics	54	26	.675	1.0	112.7	107.8	4.34
Cincinnati Royals	45	35	.563	10.0	117.8	116.6	1.03
New York Knicks	30	50	.375	25.0	116.7	119.3	-2.31
Western Division							
Los Angeles Lakers	45	35	.563	---	119.5	116.4	2.76
Baltimore Bullets	38	42	.475	7.0	118.3	119.5	-1.06
St. Louis Hawks	36	44	.450	9.0	111.4	112.0	-0.50
San Francisco Warriors	35	45	.438	10.0	115.5	118.2	-2.36
Detroit Pistons	22	58	.275	23.0	110.3	117.2	-6.07

AMERICAN HORSE OF THE YEAR
ECLIPSE AWARD

Horse	Trainer	Owner	Age	Gender
Buckpasser	Edward A Neloy	Ogden Phipps	3	C

NHL SEASON
FINAL STANDINGS

National Hockey League	GP	W	L	T	Pts	GF	GA	PIM
Chicago Black Hawks	70	41	17	12	94	264	170	757
Montreal Canadiens	70	32	25	13	77	202	188	879
Toronto Maple Leafs	70	32	27	11	75	204	211	736
New York Rangers	70	30	28	12	72	188	189	664
Detroit Red Wings	70	27	39	4	58	212	241	719
Boston Bruins	70	17	43	10	44	182	253	764

MAJOR LEAGUE BASEBALL SEASON HISTORY
American League Standings

TEAM	W	L	PCT	GB	HOME	ROAD	RS	RA	DIFF
Baltimore	97	63	.606	---	---	---	755	601	+154
Minnesota	89	73	.549	9	---	---	663	581	+82
Detroit	88	74	.543	10	---	---	719	698	+21
Chicago	83	79	.509	15	---	---	574	517	+57
Cleveland	81	81	.500	17	---	---	574	586	-12
California	80	82	.494	18	---	---	604	643	-39
Kansas City	74	86	.463	23	---	---	564	648	-84
Washington	71	88	.447	25.5	---	---	557	659	-102
Boston	72	90	.444	26	---	---	655	731	-76
New York	70	89	.438	26.5	---	---	611	612	-1

National League Standings

TEAM	W	L	PCT	GB	HOME	ROAD	RS	RA	DIFF
Los Angeles	95	67	.586	---	---	---	606	490	+116
San Francisco	93	68	.578	1.5	---	---	675	626	+49
Pittsburgh	92	70	.568	3	---	---	759	641	+118
Philadelphia	87	75	.537	8	---	---	696	640	+56
Atlanta	85	77	.521	10	---	---	782	683	+99
St. Louis	83	79	.512	12	---	---	571	577	-6
Cincinnati	76	84	.475	18	---	---	692	702	-10
Houston	72	90	.442	23	---	---	612	695	-83
New York	66	95	.410	28.5	---	---	587	761	-174
Chicago	59	103	.364	36	---	---	644	809	-165

U.S NATIONAL TENNIS CHAMPIONSHIPS

Mens Singles – Fred Stolle defeated John Newcombe
Womens Singles – Maria Bueno defeated Nancy Richey
Mens Doubles – Roy Emerson / Fred Stolle defeated Clark Graebner / Dennis Ralston
Womens Doubles – Maria Bueno / Nancy Richey defeated Billie Jean King / Rosie Casals
Mixed Doubles – Donna Floyd / Owen Davidsoon defeated Carol Hanks / Ed Rubinoff

34

1967

NATIONAL FOOTBALL LEAGUE SEASON STANDINGS

EAST	W	L	T	WEST	W	L	T
Dallas	9	5	0	Los Angeles	11	1	2
Philadelphia	6	7	1	Baltimore	11	1	2
Washington	5	6	3	San Francisco	7	7	0
New Orleans	3	11	0	Atlanta	1	12	1
Cleveland	9	5	0	Green Bay	9	4	1
NY Giants	7	7	0	Chicago	7	6	1
St. Louis	6	7	1	Detroit	5	7	2
Pittsburgh	4	9	1	Minnesota	3	8	3

U.S BADMINTON CHAMPIONSHIPS WINNERS

Mens Singles	Womens Singles	Mens Doubles	Womens Doubles	Mixed Doubles
Erland Kops	Judy Devlin	Erland Kops Joe Alston	Judy Hashman Rosine Jones Lemon	Jim Sydie Judy Hashman

NBA STANDINGS DIVISION STANDINGS

Team	W	L	W/L%	GB	PS/G	PA/G	SRS
Eastern Division							
Philadelphia 76ers	68	13	.840	-----	125.2	115.8	8.50
Boston Celtics	60	21	.741	8.0	119.3	111.3	7.24
Cincinnati Royals	39	42	.481	29.0	117.1	117.4	-0.23
New York Knicks	36	45	.444	32.0	116.4	119.4	-2.74
Baltimore Bullets	20	61	.247	48.0	115.5	122.0	-5.87
Western Division							
San Francisco Warriors	44	37	.543	---	122.4	119.5	2.58
St. Louis Hawks	39	42	.481	5.0	113.6	115.2	-1.44
Los Angeles Lakers	36	45	.444	8.0	120.5	120.2	0.31
Chicago Bulls	33	48	.407	11.0	113.2	116.9	-3.37
Detroit Pistons	30	51	.370	14.0	111.3	116.8	-4.98

AMERICAN HORSE OF THE YEAR ECLIPSE AWARD

Horse	Trainer	Owner	Age	Gender
Damascus	Frank Y. Whiteley, Jr.	Edith W. Bancroft	3	C

NHL SEASON
FINAL STANDINGS

Eastern Division	GP	W	L	T	Pts	GF	GA	PIM
Montreal Canadiens	74	42	22	10	94	236	167	700
New York Rangers	74	39	23	12	90	226	183	673
Boston Bruins	74	37	27	10	84	259	216	1043
Chicago Black Hawks	74	32	26	16	80	212	222	606
Toronto Maple Leafs	74	33	31	10	76	209	176	634
Detroit Red Wings	74	27	35	12	66	245	257	759
Western Division	**GP**	**W**	**L**	**T**	**Pts**	**GF**	**GA**	**PIM**
Philadelphia Flyers	74	31	32	11	73	173	179	987
Los Angeles Kings	74	31	33	10	72	200	224	810
St. Louis Blues	74	27	31	16	70	177	191	792
Minnesota North Stars	74	27	32	15	69	191	226	738
Pittsburgh Penguins	74	27	34	13	67	195	216	554
Oakland Seals	74	15	42	17	47	153	219	787

MAJOR LEAGUE BASEBALL SEASON HISTORY

American League Standings

TEAM	W	L	PCT	GB	HOME	ROAD	RS	RA	DIFF
Boston	92	70	.568	---	---	---	722	614	+108
Minnesota	91	71	.562	1	---	---	671	590	+81
Detroit	91	71	.562	1	---	---	683	587	+96
Chicago	89	73	.549	3	---	---	531	491	+40
California	84	77	.522	7.5	---	---	567	587	-20
Washington	76	85	.472	15.5	---	---	550	637	-87
Baltimore	76	85	.472	15.5	---	---	654	592	+62
Cleveland	75	87	.463	17	---	---	559	613	-54
New York	72	90	.444	20	---	---	522	621	-99

National League Standings

TEAM	W	L	PCT	GB	HOME	ROAD	RS	RA	DIFF
St. Louis	101	60	.627	---	---	---	695	557	+138
San Francisco	91	71	.562	10.5	---	---	652	551	+101
Chicago	87	74	.540	14	---	---	702	624	+78
Cincinnati	87	75	.537	14.5	---	---	604	563	+41
Philadelphia	82	80	.506	19.5	---	---	612	581	+31
Pittsburgh	81	81	.500	20.5	---	---	679	693	-14
Atlanta	77	85	.475	24.5	---	---	631	640	-9
Los Angeles	73	89	.451	28.5	---	---	519	595	-76

36

1968

NATIONAL FOOTBALL LEAGUE SEASON STANDINGS

EAST	W	L	T	WEST	W	L	T
Dallas	12	2	0	Baltimore	13	1	0
NY Giants	7	7	0	Los Angeles	10	3	1
Washington	5	9	0	San Francisco	7	6	1
Philadelphia	2	12	0	Atlanta	2	12	0
Cleveland	10	4	0	Minnesota	8	6	0
St. Louis	9	4	1	Chicago	7	7	0
New Orleans	4	9	1	Green Bay	6	7	1
Pittsburgh	2	11	1	Detroit	4	8	2

U.S BADMINTON CHAMPIONSHIPS WINNERS

Mens Singles	Womens Singles	Mens Doubles	Womens Doubles	Mixed Doubles
Channarong Ratanaseansuang	Tyna Barinaga	Jim Poole Don Paup	Tyna Barinaga Helen Tibbetts	Larry Saben Carlene Starkey

NBA STANDINGS DIVISION STANDINGS

Team	W	L	W/L%	GB	PS/G	PA/G	SRS
Eastern Division							
Philadelphia 76ers	62	20	.756	---	122.6	114.0	7.96
Boston Celtics	54	28	.659	8.0	116.1	112.0	3.87
New York Knicks	43	39	.524	19.0	116.1	114.3	1.78
Detroit Pistons	40	42	.488	22.0	118.6	120.6	-1.70
Cincinnati Royals	39	43	.476	23.0	116.6	117.5	-0.64
Baltimore Bullets	36	46	.439	26.0	117.4	117.8	-0.23
Western Division							
St. Louis Hawks	56	26	.683	---	113.0	110.3	2.37
Los Angeles Lakers	52	30	.634	4.0	121.2	115.6	4.99
San Francisco Warriors	43	39	.524	13.0	117.0	117.6	-0.66
Chicago Bulls	29	53	.354	27.0	109.5	113.5	-3.76
Seattle SuperSonics	23	59	.280	33.0	118.7	125.1	-6.00
San Diego Rockets	15	67	.183	41.0	112.4	121.0	-7.94

AMERICAN HORSE OF THE YEAR ECLIPSE AWARD

Horse	Trainer	Owner	Age	Gender
Dr. Fager	John A. Nerud	Tartan Stable	4	C

MAJOR LEAGUE BASEBALL SEASON HISTORY

American League Standings

TEAM	W	L	PCT	GB	HOME	ROAD	RS	RA	DIFF
Detroit	103	59	.628	---	---	---	671	492	+179
Baltimore	91	71	.562	12	---	---	579	497	+82
Cleveland	86	75	.531	16.5	---	---	516	504	+12
Boston	86	76	.531	17	---	---	614	611	+3
New York	83	79	.506	20	---	---	536	531	+5
Oakland	82	80	.503	21	---	---	569	544	+25
Minnesota	79	83	.488	24	---	---	562	546	+16
California	67	95	.414	36	---	---	498	615	-117
Chicago	67	95	.414	36	---	---	463	527	-64
Washington	65	96	.404	37.5	---	---	524	665	-141

National League Standings

TEAM	W	L	PCT	GB	HOME	ROAD	RS	RA	DIFF
St. Louis	97	65	.599	---	---	---	583	472	+111
San Francisco	88	74	.540	9	---	---	599	529	+70
Chicago	84	78	.515	13	---	---	612	611	+1
Cincinnati	83	79	.509	14	---	---	690	673	+17
Atlanta	81	81	.497	16	---	---	514	549	-35
Pittsburgh	80	82	.491	17	---	---	583	532	+51
Philadelphia	76	86	.469	21	---	---	543	615	-72
Los Angeles	76	86	.469	21	---	---	470	509	-39
New York	73	89	.448	24	---	---	473	499	-78
Houston	72	90	.444	25	---	---	510	588	-78

38

1969

NATIONAL FOOTBALL LEAGUE SEASON STANDINGS

EAST	W	L	T	WEST	W	L	T
Dallas	11	2	1	Los Angeles	11	3	0
Washington	7	5	2	Baltimore	8	5	1
New Orleans	5	9	0	Atlanta	6	8	0
Philadelphia	4	9	1	San Francisco	4	8	2
Cleveland	10	3	1	Minnesota	12	2	0
NY Giants	6	8	0	Detroit	9	4	1
St. Louis	4	9	1	Green Bay	8	6	0
Pittsburgh	1	13	0	Chicago	1	13	0

U.S BADMINTON CHAMPIONSHIPS WINNERS

Mens Singles	Womens Singles	Mens Doubles	Womens Doubles	Mixed Doubles
Rudy Hartono	Minarni	Ng Boon Bee Punch Gunalan	Minarni Retno Kustijah	Erland Kops Pernille Molgaard Hansen

NBA STANDINGS DIVISION STANDINGS

Team	W	L	W/L%	GB	PS/G	PA/G	SRS
Eastern Division							
Baltimore Bullets	57	25	.695	----	116.4	112.1	4.05
Philadelphia 76ers	55	27	.671	2.0	118.9	113.8	4.79
New York Knicks	54	28	.659	3.0	110.8	105.1	5.48
Boston Celtics	48	34	.585	9.0	111.0	105.4	5.35
Cincinnati Royals	41	41	.500	16.0	114.5	115.6	-0.83
Detroit Pistons	32	50	.390	25.0	114.1	117.3	-2.79
Miwaukee Bucks	27	55	.329	30.0	110.2	115.4	-5.07
Western Division							
Los Angeles Lakers	55	27	.671	---	112.2	108.1	3.84
Atlanta Hawks	48	34	.585	7.0	111.3	109.0	2.06
San Francisco Warriors	41	41	.500	14.0	109.1	110.7	-1.53
San Diego Rockets	37	45	.451	18.0	115.3	115.5	-0.30
Chicago Bulls	33	49	.402	22.0	104.7	107.0	-2.11
Seattle SuperSonics	30	52	.366	25.0	112.1	116.9	-4.68
Phoenix Suns	16	66	.195	39.0	111.7	120.5	-8.26

AMERICAN HORSE OF THE YEAR
ECLIPSE AWARD

Horse	Trainer	Owner	Age	Gender
Arts & Letters	J. Elliot Burch	Rokeby Stables	3	G

MAJOR LEAGUE BASEBALL SEASON HISTORY

American League Standings

TEAM	W	L	PCT	GB	HOME	ROAD	RS	RA	DIFF
Baltimore	109	53	.673	---	---	---	779	517	+262
Detroit	90	72	.556	19	---	---	701	601	+100
Boston	87	75	.537	22	---	---	743	736	+7
Washington	86	76	.531	23	---	---	694	644	+50
New York	80	81	.494	28.5	---	---	562	587	-25
Cleveland	62	99	.385	46.5	---	---	573	717	-144
Minnesota	97	65	.599	---	---	---	790	618	+172
Oakland	88	74	.543	9	---	---	740	678	+62
California	71	91	.436	26	---	---	528	652	-124
Kansas City	69	93	.423	28	---	---	586	688	-102
Chicago	68	94	.420	29	---	---	625	723	-98
Seattle	64	98	.393	33	---	---	639	799	-160

National League Standings

TEAM	W	L	PCT	GB	HOME	ROAD	RS	RA	DIFF
New York	100	62	.617	---	---	---	632	541	+91
Chicago	92	70	.564	8	---	---	720	611	+109
Pittsburgh	88	74	.543	12	---	---	725	652	+73
St. Louis	87	75	.537	13	---	---	595	540	+55
Philadelphia	63	99	.389	37	---	---	645	745	-100
Montreal	52	110	.321	48	---	---	582	791	-209
Atlanta	93	69	.574	---	---	---	691	631	+60
San Francisco	90	72	.556	3	---	---	713	636	+77
Cincinnati	89	73	.546	4	---	---	798	768	+30
Los Angeles	85	77	.525	8	---	---	645	561	+84
Houston	81	81	.500	12	---	---	676	668	+8
San Diego	52	110	.321	41	---	---	468	746	-278

1970

NATIONAL FOOTBALL LEAGUE SEASON STANDINGS

EAST	W	L	T	WEST	W	L	T
Baltimore	11	2	1	Dallas	10	4	0
Miami	10	4	0	NY Giants	9	5	0
NY Jets	4	10	0	St. Louis	8	5	1
Buffalo	3	10	1	Washington	6	8	0
Boston	2	12	0	Philadelphia	3	10	1
Cincinnati	8	6	0	Minnesota	12	2	0
Cleveland	7	7	0	Detroit	10	4	0
Pittsburgh	5	9	0	Chicago	6	8	0
Houston	3	10	1	Green Bay	6	8	0
Oakland	8	4	2	San Francisco	10	3	1
Kansas City	7	5	2	Los Angeles	9	4	1
San Diego	5	6	3	Atlanta	4	8	2
Denver	5	8	1	New Orleans	2	11	1

U.S BADMINTON CHAMPIONSHIPS WINNERS

Mens Singles	Womens Singles	Mens Doubles	Womens Doubles	Mixed Doubles
Stan Hales	Tyna Barinaga	Don Paup Jim Poole	Tyan Barinaga Caroline Hein	Jim Poole Tyna Barinaga

NBA STANDINGS DIVISION STANDINGS

Team	W	L	W/L%	GB	PS/G	PA/G	SRS
Eastern Division							
New York Knicks	60	22	.732	–	115.0	105.9	8.42
Milwaukee Bucks	56	26	.683	4.0	118.8	114.2	4.25
Baltimore Bullets	50	32	.610	10.0	120.7	118.6	1.94
Philadelphia 76ers	42	40	.512	18.0	121.9	118.5	3.32
Cincinnati Royals	36	46	.439	24.0	117.3	120.2	-2.55
Boston Celtics	34	48	.415	26.0	114.9	116.8	-1.60
Detroit Pistons	31	51	.378	29.0	112.8	116.1	-2.94
Western Division							
Atlanta Hawks	48	34	.585	---	117.6	117.2	0.31
Los Angeles Lakers	46	36	.561	2.0	113.7	111.8	1.76
Chicago Bulls	39	43	.476	9.0	114.9	116.7	-1.71
Phoenix Suns	39	43	.476	9.0	119.3	121.1	-1.66

Seattle SuperSonics	36	46	.439	12.0	116.9	119.5	-2.43
San Francisco Warriors	30	52	.366	18.0	111.1	115.6	-4.15
San Diego Rockets	27	55	.329	21.0	188.7	121.8	-2.95

AMERICAN HORSE OF THE YEAR
ECLIPSE AWARD

Horse	Trainer	Owner	Age	Gender
Fort Marcy	J. Elliot Burch	Rokeby Stables	6	G
Personality	John W. Jacobs	Ethel D. Jacobs	3	C

NHL SEASON
FINAL STANDINGS

National Hockey League	GP	W	L	T	Pts	GF	GA	PIM
Boston Bruins	78	57	14	7	121	399	207	1154
New York Rangers	78	49	18	11	109	259	177	952
Montreal Canadiens	78	42	23	13	97	291	216	1271
Toronto Maple Leafs	78	37	33	8	82	248	211	1133
Buffalo Sabres	78	24	39	15	63	217	291	1188
Vancouver Canucks	78	24	46	8	56	229	296	1371
Detroit Red Wings	78	22	45	11	55	209	308	988
Chicago Black Hawks	78	49	20	9	107	277	184	1280
St. Louis Blues	78	34	25	19	87	223	208	1092
Philadelphia Flyers	78	28	33	17	73	207	225	1060
Minnesota North Stars	78	28	34	16	72	191	223	898
Los Angeles Kings	78	25	40	13	63	239	303	775
Pittsburgh Penguins	78	21	37	20	62	221	240	1079
California Golden Seals	78	20	53	5	45	199	320	937

1971

NATIONAL FOOTBALL LEAGUE SEASON STANDINGS

EAST	W	L	T	WEST	W	L	T
Miami	10	3	1	Dallas	11	3	0
Baltimore	10	4	0	Washington	9	4	1
New England	6	8	0	Philadelphia	6	7	1
NY Jets	6	8	0	St. Louis	4	9	1
Buffalo	1	13	0	NY Giants	4	10	0
Cleveland	9	5	0	Minnesota	11	3	0
Pittsburgh	6	8	0	Detroit	7	6	1
Houston	4	9	1	Chicago	6	8	0
Cincinnati	4	10	0	Green Bay	4	8	2
Kansas City	10	3	1	San Francisco	9	5	0
Oakland	8	4	2	Los Angeles	8	5	1
San Diego	6	8	0	Atlanta	7	6	1
Denver	4	9	1	New Orleans	4	8	2

U.S BADMINTON CHAMPIONSHIPS WINNERS

Mens Singles	Womens Singles	Mens Doubles	Womens Doubles	Mixed Doubles
Stan Hales	Diane Hales	Don Paup Jim Poole	Caroline Hein Carlene Starkey	Don Paup Helen Tibbetts

NBA STANDINGS
DIVISION STANDINGS

Team	W	L	W/L%	GB	PS/G	PA/G	SRS
Atlantic Division							
New York Knicks	52	30	.634	–	110.1	105.0	5.05
Philadelphia 76ers	47	35	.573	5.0	114.8	113.3	1.81
Boston Celtics	44	8	.537	8.0	117.2	115.1	2.30
Buffalo Braves	22	60	.268	30.0	105.5	112.1	-8.02
Central Division							
Baltimore Bullets	42	40	.512	------	112.9	112.3	0.91
Atlanta Hawks	36	46	.439	6.0	114.0	115.8	-1.30
Cincinnati Royals	33	49	.402	9.0	116.0	119.2	-2.96
Cleveland Cavaliers	15	67	.183	27.0	102.1	113.3	-12.04
Midwest Division							
Milwaukee Bucks	66	16	.805	---	118.4	106.2	1192
Chicago Bulls	51	31	.622	15.0	110.6	105.4	5.47

43

Phoenix Suns	48	34	.585	18.0	113.8	111.9	2.33
Detroit Pistons	45	37	.549	21.0	110.1	110.9	-0.33
Pacific Division							
Los Angeles Lakers	48	34	.585	---	114.8	111.7	3.27
San Francisco Warriors	41	41	.500	7.0	107.1	108.5	-0.83
San Diego Rockets	40	42	.488	8.0	113.2	113.4	0.21
Seattle SuperSonics	38	44	.463	10.0	115.0	117.0	-1.53
Portland Trail Blazers	29	53	.354	19.0	115.5	120.0	-6.20

AMERICAN HORSE OF THE YEAR
ECLIPSE AWARD

Horse	Trainer	Owner	Age	Gender
Ack Ack	Charlie Whittingham	Buddy Fogelson	5	C

NHL SEASON
FINAL STANDINGS

Teams	GP	W	L	T	Pts	GF	GA	PIM
Boston Bruins	78	54	13	11	119	330	204	1112
New York Rangers	78	48	17	13	109	317	192	1010
Montreal Canadiens	78	46	16	16	108	307	205	783
Toronto Maple Leafs	78	33	31	14	80	209	208	887
Detroit Red Wings	78	33	35	10	76	261	262	850
Buffalo Sabers	78	16	43	19	51	203	289	831
Vancouver Canuck	78	20	50	8	48	203	297	1092
Chicago Black Hawks	78	46	17	15	107	256	166	844
Minnesota North Stars	78	37	29	12	86	212	191	853
St. Louis Blues	78	28	39	11	67	208	247	1150
Pittsburgh Penguins	78	26	38	14	66	220	258	978
Philadelphia Flyers	78	26	38	14	66	200	236	1233
California Golden Seals	78	21	39	18	60	216	288	1007
Loos Angeles Kings	78	20	49	9	49	206	305	719

MAJOR LEAGUE BASEBALL SEASON HISTORY
American League Standings

TEAM	W	L	PCT	GB	HOME	ROAD	RS	RA	DIFF
Baltimore	101	57	.639	---	---	---	742	530	+212
Detroit	91	71	.562	12	---	---	701	645	+56
Boston	85	77	.525	18	---	---	691	667	+24
New York	82	80	.506	21	---	---	648	641	+7
Washington	63	96	.396	38.5	---	---	537	660	-123
Cleveland	60	102	.370	43	---	---	543	747	-204

	W	L	PCT	GB	HOME	ROAD	RS	RA	DIFF
Oakland	101	60	.627	---	---	---	691	564	+127
Kansas City	85	76	.528	16	---	---	603	566	+37
Chicago	79	83	.488	22.5	---	---	617	597	+20
California	76	86	.469	25.5	---	---	511	576	-65
Minnesota	74	86	.463	26.5	---	---	654	670	-16
Milwaukee	69	92	.429	32	---	---	534	609	-75

National League Standings

TEAM	W	L	PCT	GB	HOME	ROAD	RS	RA	DIFF
Pittsburgh	97	65	.599	---	---	---	788	599	+189
St. Louis	90	72	.552	7	---	---	739	699	+40
New York	83	79	.512	14	---	---	588	550	+38
Chicago	83	79	.512	14	---	---	637	648	-11
Montreal	71	90	.438	25.5	---	---	622	729	-107
Philadelphia	67	95	.414	30	---	---	558	688	-130
San Francisco	90	72	.556	---	---	---	706	644	+62
Los Angeles	89	73	.549	1	---	---	663	587	+76
Atlanta	82	80	.506	8	---	---	643	699	-56
Houston	79	83	.488	11	---	---	585	567	+18
Cincinnati	79	83	.488	11	---	---	586	581	+5
San Diego	61	100	.379	28.5	---	---	486	610	-124

U.S NATIONAL TENNIS CHAMPIONSHIPS

Mens Singles – Stan Smith defeated Jan Kodes
Womens Singles – Billie Jean King defeated Rosemary Casals
Mens Doubles – John Newcombe / Roger Taylor defeated Stan Smith / Erik van Dillen
Womens Doubles – Rosemary Casals / Judy Tegart defeated Gail Chanfreau / Francoise Durr
Mixed Doubles – M

45

1972

NATIONAL FOOTBALL LEAGUE SEASON STANDINGS

EAST	W	L	T	WEST	W	L	T
Miami	14	0	0	Washington	11	3	0
NY Jets	7	7	0	Dallas	10	4	0
Baltimore	5	9	0	NY Giants	8	6	0
Buffalo	4	9	11	St. Louis	4	9	1
New England	3	11	0	Philadelphia	2	11	1
Pittsburgh	11	3	0	Green Bay	10	4	0
Cleveland	10	4	0	Detroit	8	5	1
Cincinnati	8	6	0	Minnesota	7	7	0
Houston	1	13	0	Chicago	4	9	1
Oakland	10	3	1	San Francisco	8	5	1
Kansas City	8	6	0	Atlanta	7	7	0
Denver	5	9	0	Los Angeles	6	7	1
San Diego	4	9	1	New Orleans	2	11	1

U.S BADMINTON CHAMPIONSHIPS WINNERS

Mens Singles	Womens Singles	Mens Doubles	Womens Doubles	Mixed Doubles
Chris Kinard	Pam Brady	Don Paup Jim Poole	P. Bretzke Pam Brady	Thomas Carmichael Pam Brady

NBA STANDINGS
DIVISION STANDINGS

Team	W	L	W/L%	GB	PS/G	PA/G	SRS
EAST							
Boston Celtics	56	26	.683	-----	115.6	110.8	4.38
New York Knicks	48	34	.585	8.0	107.1	104.7	2.28
Philadelphia 76ers	30	52	.366	26.0	112.2	115.9	-3.44
Buffalo Braves	22	60	.268	34.0	102.0	111.3	-9.44
Baltimore	38	44	.463	---	107.1	108.3	-1.26
Atlanta Hawks	36	46	.439	2.0	109.5	111.3	-1.94
Cincinnati Royals	30	52	.366	8.0	107.8	111.8	-4.13
Cleveland Cavaliers	23	59	.280	15.0	105.8	113.4	-7.90
WEST							
Milwaukee Bucks	63	19	.768	---	114.6	103.5	10.70
Chicago Bulls	57	25	.695	6.0	111.2	102.9	7.91
Phoenix Suns	49	33	.598	14.0	116.3	110.8	5.57

46

Detroit Pistons	26	56	.317	37.0	109.1	115.9	-6.11
Los Angeles Lakers	69	13	.841	---	121.0	108.7	11.65
Golden State Warriors	51	31	.622	18.0	108.2	107.4	0.92
Seattle SuperSonics	47	35	.573	22.0	109.2	108.8	0.86
Houston Rockets	34	48	.415	35.0	109.7	111.2	-1.22
Portland Trail Blazers	18	64	.220	51.0	106.8	116.5	-8.84

AMERICAN HORSE OF THE YEAR
ECLIPSE AWARD

Horse	Trainer	Owner	Age	Gender
Ack Ack	Charlie Whittingham	Buddy Fogelson	5	C

MAJOR LEAGUE BASEBALL SEASON HISTORY
American League Standings

TEAM	W	L	PCT	GB	HOME	ROAD	RS	RA	DIFF
Detroit	86	70	.551	---	---	---	558	514	+44
Boston	85	70	.548	.5	---	---	640	620	+20
Baltimore	80	74	.519	5	---	---	519	40	+89
New York	79	76	.510	6.5	---	---	557	527	+30
Cleveland	72	84	.462	14	---	---	472	519	-47
Milwaukee	65	91	.417	21	---	---	493	595	-102
Oakland	93	62	.600	---	---	---	604	457	+147
Chicago	87	67	.565	5.5	---	---	566	538	+28
Minnesota	77	77	.500	15.5	---	---	537	535	+2
Kansas City	76	78	.494	16.5	---	---	580	545	+35
California	75	80	.484	18	---	---	454	533	-79
Texas	54	100	.351	38.5	---	---	461	628	-167

National League Standings

TEAM	W	L	PCT	GB	HOME	ROAD	RS	RA	DIFF
Pittsburgh	96	59	.619	---	---	---	691	512	+179
Chicago	85	70	.545	11	---	---	685	567	+118
New York	83	73	.532	13.5	---	---	528	578	-50
St. Louis	75	81	.481	21.5	---	---	568	600	-32
Montreal	70	86	.449	26.5	---	---	513	609	-96
Philadelphia	59	97	.378	37.5	---	---	503	635	-132
Cincinnati	95	59	.617	---	---	---	707	557	+150
Houston	84	69	.549	10.5	---	---	708	636	+72
Los Angeles	85	70	.548	10.5	---	---	584	527	+57
Atlanta	70	84	.452	25	---	---	628	730	-102
San Francisco	69	86	.445	26.5	---	---	662	649	+13

47

1973

U.S BADMINTON CHAMPIONSHIPS
WINNERS

Mens Singles	Womens Singles	Mens Doubles	Womens Doubles	Mixed Doubles
Sture Johnsson	Eva Twedberg	Jim Poole Don Paup	Pam Brady Diane Hales	Sture Johnsson Eva Twedberg

NBA STANDINGS
DIVISION STANDINGS

Team	W	L	W/L%	GB	PS/G	PA/G	SRS
Eastern Division							
Boston Celtics	68	14	.829	–	112.7	104.5	7.35
New York Knicks	57	25	.695	11.0	105.0	98.2	6.07
Buffalo Braves	21	61	.256	47.0	103.3	112.5	-8.85
Philadelphia 76ers	9	73	.110	59.0	104.1	116.2	-11.50
Baltimore Bullets	52	30	.634	---	105.0	101.6	2.85
Atlanta Hawks	46	36	.561	6.0	112.4	112.3	-0.15
Houston Rockets	33	49	.402	19.0	112.8	114.5	-1.81
Cleveland Cavaliers	32	50	.390	20.0	102.7	105.3	-2.64
Western Division							
Milwaukee Bucks	60	22	.732	---	107.2	99.0	7.84
Chicago Bulls	51	31	.622	9.0	104.1	100.6	3.43
Detroit Pistons	40	42	.488	20.0	110.3	110.0	0.54
Kansas City Omaha Kings	36	46	.439	24.0	107.6	110.5	-2.36
Los Angeles Lakers	60	22	.732	---	111.7	103.2	8.16
Golden State Warriors	47	35	.573	13.0	108.8	105.7	3.12
Phoenix Suns	38	44	.463	22.0	111.6	112.9	-0.96
Seattle SuperSonics	26	56	.317	34.0	103.7	109.6	-5.33
Portland Trail Blazers	21	61	.256	39.0	106.2	112.4	-5.67

AMERICAN HORSE OF THE YEAR
ECLIPSE AWARD

Horse	Trainer	Owner	Age	Gender
Secretariat	Lucien Laurin	Meadow Stable	3	C

NHL SEASON
FINAL STANDINGS

Team	GP	W	L	T	Pts	GF	GA	PIM
Boston Bruins	78	52	17	9	113	349	221	968
Montreal Canadiens	78	45	24	9	99	293	240	761
New York Rangers	78	40	24	14	94	300	251	782

Toronto Maple Leafs	78	35	27	16	86	274	230	903
Buffalo Sabres	78	32	34	12	76	242	250	787
Detroit Red Wings	78	29	39	10	68	255	319	917
Vancouver Canucks	78	24	43	11	59	224	296	952
New York Islanders	78	19	41	18	56	182	247	1075
Philadelphia Flyers	78	50	16	12	112	273	164	1750
Chicago Black Hawks	78	41	14	23	105	272	164	877
Los Angeles Kings	78	33	33	12	78	233	231	1055
Atlanta Flames	78	30	34	14	74	214	238	841
Pittsburgh Penguins	78	28	41	9	65	242	273	950
St. Louis Blues	78	26	40	12	64	206	248	1147
Minnesota North Stars	78	23	38	17	63	235	275	821
California Golden Seals	78	13	55	10	36	195	342	651

MAJOR LEAGUE BASEBALL SEASON HISTORY

American League Standings

TEAM	W	L	PCT	GB	HOME	ROAD	RS	RA	DIFF
Baltimore	97	65	.599	---	---	---	754	561	+193
Boston	89	73	.549	8	---	---	738	647	+91
Detroit	85	77	.525	12	---	---	642	674	-32
New York	80	82	.494	17	---	---	641	610	+31
Milwaukee	74	88	.457	23	---	---	708	731	-23
Cleveland	71	91	.438	26	---	---	680	826	-146
Oakland	94	68	.580	---	---	---	758	615	+143
Kansas City	88	74	.543	6	---	---	755	752	+3
Minnesota	81	81	.500	13	---	---	738	692	+46
California	79	83	.488	15	---	---	629	657	-28
Chicago	77	85	.475	17	---	---	652	705	-53
Texas	57	105	.352	37	---	---	619	844	-225

National League Standings

TEAM	W	L	PCT	GB	HOME	ROAD	RS	RA	DIFF
New York	82	79	.509	---	---	---	608	588	+20
St. Louis	81	81	.500	1.5	---	---	643	603	+40
Pittsburgh	80	82	.494	2.5	---	---	704	693	+11
Montreal	79	83	.488	3.5	---	---	668	702	-34
Chicago	77	84	.478	5	---	---	614	655	-41
Philadelphia	71	91	.438	11.5	---	---	642	717	-75
Cincinnati	99	63	.611	---	---	---	741	621	+120
Los Angeles	95	66	.586	3.5	---	---	675	565	+110

49

1974

NATIONAL FOOTBALL LEAGUE SEASON
STANDINGS

EAST	W	L	T	WEST	W	L	T
Miami	11	3	0	St. Louis	10	4	0
Buffalo	9	5	0	Washington	10	4	0
New England	7	7	0	Dallas	8	6	0
NY Jets	7	7	0	Philadelphia	7	7	0
Baltimore	2	12	0	NY Giants	2	12	0
Pittsburgh	10	3	1	Minnesota	10	4	0
Cincinnati	7	7	0	Detroit	7	7	0
Houston	7	7	0	Green Bay	6	8	0
Cleveland	4	10	0	Chicago	4	10	0
Oakland	12	2	0	Los Angeles	10	4	0
Denver	7	6	1	San Francisco	6	8	0
Kansas City	5	9	0	New Orleans	5	9	0
San Diego	5	9	0	Atlanta	3	11	0

U.S BADMINTON CHAMPIONSHIPS
WINNERS

Mens Singles	Womens Singles	Mens Doubles	Womens Doubles	Mixed Doubles
Chris Kinard	Cindy Baker	Don Paup Jim Poole	Pam Brady Diane Hales	Mike Walker Judianne Kelly

NBA STANDINGS
DIVISION STANDINGS

Team	W	L	W/L%	GB	PS/G	PA/G	SRS
East							
Boston Celtics	56	26	.683	-----	109.0	105.1	3.42
New York Knicks	49	33	.598	7.0	101.3	98.5	2.42
Buffalo Braves	42	40	.512	14.0	111.6	111.8	-0.19
Philadelphia 76ers	25	57	.305	31.0	101.2	107.5	-5.94
Capital Bullets	47	35	.573	---	101.9	100.4	1.19
Atlanta Hawks	35	47	.427	12.0	108.6	110.0	-1.47
Houston Rockets	32	50	.390	15.0	107.4	107.6	-0.34
Cleveland Cavaliers	29	53	.354	18.0	100.3	104.6	-4.16
West							
Milwaukee Bucks	59	23	.720	---	107.1	99.0	7.61
Chicago Bulls	54	28	.659	5.0	102.0	98.7	3.20
Detroit Pistons	52	30	.634	7.0	104.4	100.3	4.02

Kansas City Omaha Kings	33	49	.402	26.0	102.0	105.8	-3.24
Los Angeles Lakers	47	35	.573	---	109.2	108.3	0.85
Golden State Warriors	44	38	.537	3.0	109.9	107.3	2.42
Seattle SuperSonics	36	46	.439	11.0	107.0	109.5	-2.29
Phoenix Suns	30	52	3.66	17.0	107.9	111.5	-3.20
Portland Trail Blazers	27	55	.329	20.0	106.8	111.6	-4.30

AMERICAN HORSE OF THE YEAR
ECLIPSE AWARD

Horse	Trainer	Owner	Age	Gender
Forego	Sherrill W. Ward	Lazy F. Ranch	4	G

MAJOR LEAGUE BASEBALL SEASON HISTORY

American League Standings

TEAM	W	L	PCT	GB	HOME	ROAD	RS	RA	DIFF
Baltimore	91	71	.562	------	------	------	659	612	+47
New York	89	73	.549	2	------	------	671	623	+48
Boston	84	78	.519	7	---	---	696	661	+35
Cleveland	77	85	.475	14	---	---	662	694	-32
Milwaukee	76	86	.469	15	---	---	647	660	-13
Detroit	72	90	.444	19	---	---	620	768	-148
Oakland	90	72	.556	–	---	---	689	551	+138
Texas	84	76	.522	5	---	---	690	698	-8
Minnesota	82	80	.503	8	---	---	673	669	+4
Chicago	80	80	.491	9	---	---	684	721	-37
Kansas City	77	85	.475	13	---	---	667	662	+5
California	68	94	.417	22	---	---	618	657	-39

National League Standings

TEAM	W	L	PCT	GB	HOME	ROAD	RS	RA	DIFF
Pittsburgh	88	74	.543	---	---	---	751	657	+94
St. Louis	86	75	.534	1.5	---	---	677	643	+34
Philadelphia	80	82	.494	8	---	---	676	701	-25
Montreal	79	82	.491	8.5	---	---	662	657	+5
New York	71	91	.438	17	---	---	572	646	-74
Chicago	66	96	.407	22	---	---	669	826	-157
Los Angeles	102	60	.630	---	---	---	798	561	+237
Cincinnati	98	64	.601	4	---	---	776	631	+145
Atlanta	88	74	.540	14	---	---	661	563	+98
Houston	81	81	.500	21	---	---	653	632	+21

San Francisco	72	90	.444	30	---	---	634	723	-89
San Diego	60	102	.370	42	---	---	541	830	-289

U.S NATIONAL TENNIS CHAMPIONSHIPS

Mens Singles – Jimmy Connors defeated Ken Rosewall
Womens Singles – Billie Jean King defeated Evonne Goolagong
Mens Doubles – Bob Lutz / Stan Smith defeated Patricio Cornejo / Jaime Fillol
Womens Doubles – Rosemary Casals / Billie Jean King defeated Francoise Durr / Betty Stove
Mixed Doubles – Pam Teeguarden / Geoff Masters defeated Chris Evert / Jimmy Connors

52

1975

U.S BADMINTON CHAMPIONSHIPS
WINNERS

Mens Singles	Womens Singles	Mens Doubles	Womens Doubles	Mixed Doubles
Mike Adams	Judianne Kelly	Don Paup Jim Poole	Diane Hales Carlene Starkey	Mike Walker Judianne Kelly

NBA STANDINGS
DIVISION STANDINGS

Team	W	L	W/L%	GB	PS/G	PA/G	SRS
East							
Boston Celtics	60	22	.732	--	106.5	100.8	5.40
Buffalo Braves	49	3	.598	11.0	107.8	105.6	2.16
New York Knicks	40	42	.488	20.0	100.4	101.7	-0.92
Philadelphia 76ers	34	48	.415	26.0	99.8	102.8	-2.60
Washington Bullets	60	22	.732	---	104.7	97.5	6.53
Houston Rockets	41	41	.500	19.0	103.9	102.9	0.84
Cleveland Cavaliers	40	42	.488	20.0	99.0	99.4	-0.31
Atlanta Hawks	31	51	.378	29.0	105.1	106.5	-1.32
New Orleans Jazz	23	59	.280	37.0	101.5	109.3	-7.30
West							
Chicago Bulls	47	35	.573	---	98.1	95.0	2.88
Kansas City Ohama Kings	44	38	.537	3.0	101.4	101.6	-0.16
Detroit Pistons	40	42	.488	7.0	98.9	100.3	-1.19
Milwaukee Bucks	38	44	.463	9.0	100.7	100.5	0.25
Golden State Warriors	48	34	.585	---	108.5	105.2	2.86
Seattle SuperSonics	43	39	.524	5.0	103.1	104.1	-1.19
Portland Trail Blazers	38	44	.463	10.0	103.8	103.3	0.27
Phoenix Suns	32	50	.390	16.0	101.2	103.6	-2.36
Los Angeles Lakers	30	52	.366	18.0	103.2	107.2	-3.94

AMERICAN HORSE OF THE YEAR
ECLIPSE AWARD

Horse	Trainer	Owner	Age	Gender
Forego	Sherrill W. Ward	Lazy F. Ranch	5	G

MAJOR LEAGUE BASEBALL SEASON HISTORY
American League Standings

TEAM	W	L	PCT	GB	HOME	ROAD	RS	RA	DIFF
Boston	95	65	.594	---	---	---	796	709	+87
Baltimore	90	69	.566	4.5	---	---	682	553	+129

New York	83	77	.519	12	---	---	681	588	+93
Cleveland	79	80	.497	15.5	---	---	688	703	-15
Milwaukee	68	94	.420	28	---	---	675	792	-117
Detroit	57	102	.358	37.5	---	---	570	786	-216
Oakland	98	64	.605	---	---	---	758	606	+152
Kansas City	91	71	.562	7	---	---	710	649	+61
Texas	79	83	.488	19	---	---	714	733	-19
Minnesota	76	83	.478	20.5	---	---	724	736	-12
Chicago	75	86	.466	22.5	---	---	655	703	-48
California	72	89	.447	25.5	—	---	628	723	-95

National League Standings

TEAM	W	L	PCT	GB	HOME	ROAD	RS	RA	DIFF
Pittsburgh	92	69	.571	---	---	---	712	565	+147
Philadelphia	86	76	.531	6.5	---	---	735	694	+41
New York	82	80	.506	10.5	---	---	646	625	+21
St. Louis	82	80	.503	10.5	---	---	662	689	-27
Montreal	75	87	.463	17.5	---	---	601	690	-89
Chicago	75	87	.463	17.5	---	---	712	827	-115
Cincinnati	108	54	.667	---	---	---	840	586	+254
Los Angeles	88	74	.543	20	---	---	648	534	+114
San Francisco	80	81	.497	27.5	---	---	659	671	-12
San Diego	71	91	.438	37	---	---	552	683	-131
Atlanta	67	94	.416	40.5	---	---	583	739	-156
Houston	64	97	.395	43.5	---	---	664	711	-47

U.S NATIONAL TENNIS CHAMPIONSHIPS

Mens Singles – Manuel Orantes defeated Jimmy Connors
Womens Singles – Chris Evert defeated Evonne Goolagong Cawley
Mens Doubles – Jimmy Connors / Ilie Nastase defeated Tom Okker / Marty Riesen
Womens Doubles – Margaret Court / Virginia Wade deafeted Rosemary Casals / Bille Jean King
Mixed Doubles – Rosemary Casals / Dick Stockton defeated Billie Jean King / Fred Stolle

54

1976

NATIONAL FOOTBALL LEAGUE SEASON STANDINGS

Team	W	L	T	Team	W	L	T
Baltimore	11	3	0	Dallas	11	3	0
New England	11	3	0	Washington	10	4	0
Miami	6	8	0	St. Louis	10	4	0
NY Jets	3	11	0	Philadelphia	4	10	0
Buffalo	2	12	0	NY Giants	3	11	0
Pittsburgh	10	4	0	Minnesota	11	2	1
Cincinnati	10	4	0	Chicago	7	7	0
Cleveland	9	5	0	Detroit	6	8	0
Houston	5	9	0	Green Bay	5	9	0
Oakland	13	1	0	Los Angeles	10	3	1
Denver	9	5	0	San Francisco	8	6	0
San Diego	6	8	0	Atlanta	4	10	0
Kansas City	5	9	0	New Orleans	4	10	0
Tampa Bay	0	14	0	Seattle	2	12	0

U.S BADMINTON CHAMPIONSHIPS WINNERS

Mens Singles	Womens Singles	Mens Doubles	Womens Doubles	Mixed Doubles
Chris Kinard	Pam Brady	Don Paup Bruce Pontow	Pam Brady Rosine Lemon	Mike Walker Judianne Kelly

NBA STANDINGS DIVISION STANDINGS

Team	W	L	W/L%	GB	PS/G	PA/G	SRS
East							
Boston Celtics	54	28	.659	–	106.2	103.9	2.25
Philadelphia 76ers	46	36	.561	8.0	106.5	106.3	0.33
Buffalo Braves	46	36	.561	8.0	107.3	106.4	0.85
New York Knicks	38	44	.463	16.0	102.7	103.9	-1.05
Cleveland Cavaliers	49	33	.598	---	101.7	99.2	2.34
Washington Bullets	48	34	.585	1.0	102.8	100.4	2.20
Houston Rockets	40	42	.488	9.0	106.2	107.0	-0.71
New Orleans Jazz	38	44	.463	11.0	104.1	105.0	-0.74
Atlanta Hawks	29	53	.354	20.0	102.6	105.5	-2.66
West							
Milwaukee Bucks	38	44	.463	------	101.8	103.3	-1.55

Detroit Pistons	36	46	.439	2.0	104.9	106.0	-1.18
Kansas City Kings	31	51	.378	7.0	103.3	106.2	-2.83
Chicago Bulls	24	58	.293	14.0	95.9	98.8	-2.89
Golden State Warriors	59	23	.720	---	109.8	103.1	6.23
Seattle SuperSonics	43	39	.524	16.0	106.4	106.7	-0.15
Phoenix Suns	42	40	.512	17.0	105.1	104.5	0.59
Los Angeles Lakers	40	42	.488	19.0	106.9	106.8	0.18
Portland Trail Blazers	37	45	.451	22.0	104.1	105.3	-1.11

AMERICAN HORSE OF THE YEAR
ECLIPSE AWARD

Horse	Trainer	Owner	Age	Gender
Forego	Frank Y. Whiteley, Jr.	Lazy F. Ranch	6	G

MAJOR LEAGUE BASEBALL SEASON HISTORY

American League Standings

TEAM	W	L	PCT	GB	HOME	ROAD	RS	RA	DIFF
New York	97	62	.610	---	---	---	730	575	+155
Baltimore	88	74	.543	10.5	---	---	619	598	+21
Boston	83	79	.512	15.5	---	---	716	660	+56
Cleveland	81	78	.509	16	---	---	615	615	0
Detroit	74	87	.460	24	---	---	609	709	-100
Milwaukee	66	95	.410	32	---	---	570	655	-85
Kansas City	90	72	.556	---	---	---	713	611	+102
Oakland	87	74	.540	2.5	---	---	686	598	+88
Minnesota	85	77	.525	5	---	---	743	704	+39
Texas	76	86	.469	14	---	---	616	652	-36
California	76	86	.469	14	---	---	550	631	-81
Chicago	64	97	.398	25.5	---	---	586	745	-159

National League Standings

TEAM	W	L	PCT	GB	HOME	ROAD	RS	RA	DIFF
Philadelphia	101	61	6.23	---	---	---	770	557	+213
Pittsburgh	92	70	.568	9	---	---	708	630	+78
New York	86	76	.531	15	---	---	615	538	+77
Chicago	75	87	.463	26	---	---	611	728	-117
St. Louis	72	90	.444	29	---	---	629	671	-42
Montreal	55	107	.340	46	---	---	531	734	-203
Cincinnati	102	60	.630	---	---	—	857	633	+224
Los Angeles	92	70	.568	10	---	---	608	543	+65
Houston	80	82	.494	22	---	---	625	657	-32

San Francisco	74	88	.457	28	---	---	595	686	-91
San Diego	73	89	.451	29	---	---	570	662	-92
Atlanta	70	92	.432	32	---	---	620	700	-80

U.S NATIONAL TENNIS CHAMPIONSHIPS

Mens Singles – Jimmy Connors defeated Bjorn Borg
Womens Singles – Chris Evert defeated Evonne Goolagong
Mens Doubles – Tom Okker / Marty Riessen defeated Paul Kronk / Cliff Letcher
Womens Doubles – Delina Boshoff / Ilana Kloss defeated Olga Morozova / Virginia Wade
Mixed Doubles – Billie Jean King / Phil Dent defeated Betty Stove / Frew McMillan

1977

NATIONAL FOOTBALL LEAGUE SEASON STANDINGS

EAST	W	L	T	WEST	W	L	T
Baltimore	10	4	0	Denver	12	2	0
Miami	10	4	0	Oakland	11	3	0
New England	9	5	0	San Diego	7	7	0
NY Jets	3	11	0	Seattle	5	9	0
Buffalo	3	11	0	Kansas City	2	12	0
Dallas	12	2	0	Los Angeles	10	4	0
Washington	9	5	0	Atlanta	7	7	0
St. Louis	7	7	0	San Francisco	5	9	0
Philadelphia	5	9	0	New Orleans	3	11	0
NY Giants	5	9	0				

U.S BADMINTON CHAMPIONSHIPS WINNERS

Mens Singles	Womens Singles	Mens Doubles	Womens Doubles	Mixed Doubles
Chris Kinard	Pam Brady	Jim Poole Mike Walker	Diana Osterhues Janet Wilts	Bruce Ponotow Pam Brady

NBA STANDINGS DIVISION STANDINGS

Team	W	L	W/L%	GB	PS/G	PA/G	SRS
East							
Philadelphia 76ers	30	52	.610	–	110.2	106.2	3.78
Boston Celtics	44	38	.537	6.0	104.5	106.5	-1.90
New York Knick	40	42	.488	10.0	108.6	108.6	0.01
Buffalo Braves	30	52	.366	20.0	105.0	109.5	.4.28
New York Nets	22	60	2.68	28.0	95.9	102.7	-6.54
Houston Rockets	49	33	.268	28.0	95.9	102.7	-6.54
Washington Bullets	48	34	.585	1.0	105.5	104.5	0.90
San Antonio Spurs	44	38	.537	5.0	115.0	114.4	0.53
Cleveland Cavaliers	43	39	.524	6.0	102.1	101.0	1.08
New Orleans Jazz	35	47	.427	14.0	104.6	107.4	-2.68
Atlanta Hawks	31	51	.378	18.0	102.4	106.4	-3.87
West							
Denver Nuggets	50	32	.610	----	112.6	107.4	4.95
Detroit Pistons	44	38	.537	6.0	109.4	110.4	-1.00
Chicago Bulls	44	38	.537	6.0	98.9	98.0	0.92

Kansas City Kings	40	42	.488	10.0	107.7	106.8	0.93
Indian Pacers	36	46	.439	14.0	106.8	108.6	-1.68
Milwaukee Bucks	30	52	.366	20.0	108.4	111.5	-2.99
Los Angeles Lakers	53	29	.646	---	106.9	104.1	2.64
Portland Trail Blazers	49	33	.598	4.0	111.7	106.2	5.39
Golden State Warriors	46	36	.561	7.0	110.9	107.7	3.10
Seattle SuperSonics	40	42	.488	13.0	104.0	105.5	-1.43
Phoenix Suns	34	48	.415	19.0	104.9	104.2	0.64

AMERICAN HORSE OF THE YEAR
ECLIPSE AWARD

Horse	Trainer	Owner	Age	Gender
Seattle Slew	William H Turner Jr	Karen & Mickey Taylor	3	C

MAJOR LEAGUE BASEBALL SEASON HISTORY

American League Standings

TEAM	W	L	PCT	GB	HOME	ROAD	RS	RA	DIFF
New York	100	62	.617	------	------	------	831	651	+180
Baltimore	97	64	.602	2.5	---	---	719	653	+66
Boston	97	64	.602	2.5	---	---	859	712	+147
Detroit	74	88	.457	26	---	---	714	751	-37
Cleveland	71	90	.441	28.5	---	---	676	739	-63
Milwaukee	67	95	.414	33	---	---	639	765	-126
Toronto	54	107	.335	45.5	---	---	605	822	-217
Kansas City	102	60	.630	---	---	---	822	651	+171
Texas	94	68	.580	8	---	---	767	657	+110
Chicago	90	72	.556	12	---	---	844	771	+73
Minnesota	84	77	.522	17.5	---	---	867	776	+91
California	74	88	.457	28	---	---	675	695	-20
Seattle	64	98	.395	38	---	---	624	855	-231
Oakland	63	98	.391	38.5	---	---	605	749	-144

National League Standings

TEAM	W	L	PCT	GB	HOME	ROAD	RS	RA	DIFF
Philadelphia	101	61	.623	---	---	---	847	668	+179
Pittsburgh	96	66	.593	5	---	---	734	665	+69
St. Louis	83	79	.512	18	---	---	737	688	+49
Chicago	81	81	.500	20	---	---	692	739	-47
Montreal	75	87	.463	26	---	---	665	736	-71
New York	64	98	.395	37	---	---	587	663	-76
Los Angeles	98	64	.605	---	---	---	769	582	+187

59

Cincinnati	88	74	.543	10	---	---	802	725	+77
Houston	81	81	.500	17	---	---	680	650	+30
San Francisco	75	87	.463	23	---	---	673	711	-38
San Diego	69	93	.426	29	---	---	692	834	-142
Atlanta	61	101	.377	37	---	---	678	895	-217

U.S NATIONAL TENNIS CHAMPIONSHIPS

Mens Singles – Guillermo Vilas defeated Jimmy Connors
Womens Singles – Chris Evert defeated Wendy Turnball
Mens Doubles – Bob Hewiitt / Frew McMillan defeated Brian Gottfried / Raul Ramirez
Womens Doubles – Martina Navratilove / Betty Stove defeated Renee Richards / Betty-Ann Stuart
Mixed Doubles – Betty Stove / Frew McMillan defeated Billie Jean King / Vitas Gerulaitus

60

1978

NATIONAL FOOTBALL LEAGUE SEASON
STANDINGS

EAST	W	L	T	WEST	W	L	T
New England	11	5	0	Denver	10	6	0
Miami	11	5	0	San Diego	9	7	0
Dallas	12	4	0	Seattle	9	7	0
Philadelphia	9	7	0	Oakland	9	7	0
NY Jets	8	8	0	Kansas City	4	12	0
Washington	8	8	0	Los Angeles	12	4	0
Buffalo	5	11	0	Atlanta	9	7	0
St. Louis	6	10	0	New Orleans	7	9	0
Baltimore	5	11	0	San Francisco	2	14	0
NY Giants	6	10	0				

U.S BADMINTON CHAMPIONSHIPS
WINNERS

Mens Singles	Womens Singles	Mens Doubles	Womens Doubles	Mixed Doubles
Mike Walker	Cheryl Carton	John Britton Charles Coakley	Diana Osterhues Janet Wilts	Bruce Pontow Pam Brady

NBA STANDINGS
DIVISION STANDINGS

Team	W	L	W/L%	GB	PS/G	PA/G	SRS
East							
Philadelphia 76ers	55	27	.671	–	114.7	109.6	4.87
New York Knicks	43	39	.524	12.0	113.4	114.0	-0.53
Boston Celtics	32	50	.390	23.0	105.7	107.7	-1.86
Buffalo Braves	27	55	.329	28.0	105.3	109.0	-3.55
New Jersey Nets	24	58	.293	31.0	106.7	112.5	-5.61
San Antonio Spurs	52	30	.634	---	114.5	111.1	3.20
Washington Bullets	44	38	.537	8.0	110.3	109.4	0.82
Cleveland Cavaliers	43	39	.524	9.0	104.4	103.9	0.44
Atlanta Hawks	41	41	.500	11.0	103.7	103.9	-0.13
New Orleans Jazz	39	43	.476	13.0	107.6	109.5	-1.80
Houston Rockets	28	54	.341	24.0	103.8	107.8	-3.83
West							
Denver Nuggets	48	34	.585	------	111.8	110.9	0.80
Milwaukee Bucks	44	38	.537	4.0	112.4	113.0	-0.59
Chicago Bulls	40	42	.488	8.0	103.9	104.8	-0.79

Detroit Pistons	38	44	.463	10.0	109.0	110.2	-1.22
Kansas City Kings	31	51	.378	17.0	109.5	111.4	-1.76
Indiana Pacers	31	51	.378	17.0	108.6	111.1	-2.37
Portland Trail Blazers	58	24	.707	---	107.7	101.5	5.92
Phoenix Suns	49	33	.598	9.0	112.3	108.6	3.50
Seattle SuperSonics	47	35	.573	11.0	104.5	102.9	1.48
Los Angeles Lakers	45	37	.549	13.0	110.3	107.6	2.59
Golden State Warriors	43	39	.524	15.0	106.1	105.7	0.41

AMERICAN HORSE OF THE YEAR
ECLIPSE AWARD

Horse	Trainer	Owner	Age	Gender
Affirmed	Laz Barrera	Harbor View Frm	3	C

MAJOR LEAGUE BASEBALL SEASON HISTORY
American League Standings

TEAM	W	L	PCT	GB	HOME	ROAD	RS	RA	DIFF
New York	100	63	.613	---	---	---	735	582	+153
Boston	99	64	.607	1	---	---	796	657	+139
Milwaukee	93	69	.574	6.5	---	---	804	650	+154
Baltimore	90	71	.559	9	---	---	659	633	+26
Detroit	86	76	.531	13.5	---	---	714	653	+61
Cleveland	69	90	.434	29	---	---	639	694	-55
Toronto	59	102	.366	40	---	---	590	775	-185
Kansas City	92	70	.568	---	---	---	743	634	+109
Texas	87	75	.537	5	---	---	692	632	+60
California	87	75	.537	5	---	---	691	666	+25
Minnesota	73	89	.451	19	---	---	666	678	-12
Chicago	71	90	.441	20.5	---	---	634	731	-97
Oakland	69	93	.426	23	---	---	532	690	-158
Seattle	56	104	.350	35	---	---	614	834	-220

National League Standings

TEAM	W	L	PCT	GB	HOME	ROAD	RS	RA	DIFF
Philadelphia	90	72	.556	---	---	---	708	586	+122
Pittsburgh	88	73	.547	1.5	---	---	684	637	+47
Chicago	79	83	.488	11	---	---	664	724	-60
Montreal	76	86	.469	14	---	---	633	611	+22
St. Louis	69	93	.426	21	---	---	600	657	-57
New York	66	96	.407	24	---	---	607	690	-83
Los Angeles	95	67	.586	---	---	---	727	573	+154

Cincinnati	92	69	.571	2.5	---	---	710	688	+22
San Francisco	89	73	.549	6	---	---	613	594	+19
San Diego	84	78	.519	11	---	---	591	598	-7
Houston	74	88	.457	21	---	---	605	634	-29
Atlanta	69	93	.426	26	---	---	600	750	-150

U.S NATIONAL TENNIS CHAMPIONSHIPS

Mens Singles – Jimmy Connors defeated Bjorn Borg
Womens Singles – Chris Evert defeated Pam Shriver
Mens Doubles – Bob Lutz / Stan Smith defeated Marty Riessen / Sherwood Stewart
Womens Doubles – Billie Jean King / Martina Navratilova defeated Kerry Melville Reid / Wendy Turnball
Mixed Doubles – Betty Stove / Frew McMillian defeated Billie Jean King / Ray Ruffels

63

1979

NATIONAL FOOTBALL LEAGUE SEASON STANDINGS

EAST	W	L	T	WEST	W	L	T
Miami	10	6	0	San Diego	12	4	0
New England	9	7	0	Denver	10	6	0
NY Jets	8	8	0	Seattle	9	7	0
Buffalo	7	9	0	Oakland	9	7	0
Baltimore	5	11	0	Kansas City	7	9	0
Dallas	11	5	0	Los Angeles	9	7	0
Philadelphia	11	5	0	New Orleans	8	8	0
Washington	10	6	0	Atlanta	6	10	0
NY Giants	6	10	0	San Francisco	2	14	0

U.S BADMINTON CHAMPIONSHIPS WINNERS

Mens Singles	Womens Singles	Mens Doubles	Womens Doubles	Mixed Doubles
Chris Kinard	Pam Brady	Jim Poole Mike Walker	Pam Brady Judianne King	Mike Walker Judianne Kelly

NBA STANDINGS
DIVISION STANDINGS

Team	W	L	W/L%	GB	PS/G	PA/G	SRS
East							
Washington Bullets	54	28	.659	-----	114.9	109.9	4.75
Philadelphia 76ers	47	35	.573	7.0	109.5	107.7	1.74
New Jersey Nets	37	45	.451	17.0	107.7	111.9	-4.00
New York Knicks	31	51	.378	23.0	107.7	111.1	-3.29
Boston Celtics	29	53	.354	25.0	108.2	113.3	-4.78
San Antonio Spurs	48	34	.585	---	119.3	114.1	4.97
Houston Rockets	47	35	.573	1.0	113.4	112.4	0.92
Atlanta Hawks	46	36	.561	2.0	109.1	107.1	1.92
Detroit Pistons	30	52	.366	18.0	110.0	112.7	-2.60
Cleveland Cavaliers	30	52	.366	18.0	106.5	110.2	-3.57
New Orleans Jazz	26	56	.317	22.0	108.3	114.6	-5.97
West							
Kansas City Kings	48	34	.585	---	113.1	110.2	2.73
Denver Nuggets	47	35	.573	1.0	110.7	109.5	1.24
Milwaukee Bucks	38	44	.463	10.0	114.1	111.8	2.12
Indiana Pacers	38	44	.463	10.0	108.6	110.2	-1.41

Chicago Bulls	31	51	.378	17.0	104.7	108.7	-3.78
Seattle SuperSonics	52	30	.634	---	106.6	103.9	2.69
Phoenix Suns	50	32	.610	2.0	115.4	111.7	3.55
Los Angeles Lakers	47	35	.573	5.0	112.9	109.9	2.95
Portland Trail Blazers	45	37	.549	7.0	108.4	107.1	1.12
San Diego Clippers	43	39	.524	9.0	113.1	114.9	-1.76
Golden State Warriors	38	44	.463	14.0	105.1	104.8	0.46

AMERICAN HORSE OF THE YEAR
ECLIPSE AWARD

Horse	Trainer	Owner	Age	Gender
Affirmed	Laz Barrera	Harbor View Farm	4	C

MAJOR LEAGUE BASEBALL SEASON HISTORY

American League Standings

TEAM	W	L	PCT	GB	HOME	ROAD	RS	RA	DIFF
Baltimore	102	57	.642	---	---	---	757	582	+175
Milwaukee	95	66	.590	8	---	---	807	722	+85
Boston	91	69	.569	11.5	---	---	841	711	+130
New York	89	71	.556	13.5	---	---	734	672	+62
Detroit	85	76	.528	18	---	---	770	738	+32
Cleveland	81	80	.503	22	---	---	760	805	-45
Toronto	53	109	.327	50.5	---	---	613	862	-249
California	88	74	.543	---	---	---	866	768	+98
Kansas City	85	77	.525	3	---	---	851	816	+35
Texas	83	79	.512	5	---	---	750	698	+52
Minnesota	82	80	.506	6	---	---	764	725	+39
Chicago	73	87	.456	14	---	---	730	748	-18
Seattle	67	95	.414	21	---	---	711	820	-109
Oakland	54	108	.333	34	---	---	573	860	-287

National League Standings

TEAM	W	L	PCT	GB	HOME	ROAD	RS	RA	DIFF
Pittsburgh	98	64	.601	---	---	---	775	643	+132
Montreal	95	65	.594	2	---	---	701	581	+120
St. Louis	86	76	.528	12	---	---	731	693	+38
Philadelphia	84	78	.515	14	---	---	683	718	-35
Chicago	80	82	.494	18	---	---	706	707	-1
New York	63	99	.387	35	---	---	593	706	-113
Cincinnati	90	71	.559	---	---	---	731	644	+87
Houston	89	73	.549	1.5	---	---	583	582	+1

65

Los Angeles	79	83	.488	11.5	---	---	739	717	+22
San Francisco	71	91	.438	19.5	---	---	672	751	-79
San Diego	68	93	.422	22	---	---	603	681	-78
Atlanta	66	94	.413	23.5	---	---	669	763	-94

U.S NATIONAL TENNIS CHAMPIONSHIPS

Mens Singles – John McEnroe defeated Vitas Geralaitis
Womens Singles – Tracy Austin defeated Chris Evert
Mens Doubles – John McEnroe / Peter Fleming defeated Bob Lutz / Stan Smith
Womens Doubles – Betty Stove / Wendy Turnball defeated Billie Jean King / Martina Navratilova
Mixed Doubles – Greer Stevens / Bob Hewitt defeated Betty Stove / Frew McMillan

1980

EAST	W	L	T	WEST	W	L	T
Buffalo	11	5	0	San Diego	11	5	0
New England	10	6	0	Oakland	11	5	0
Miami	8	8	0	Kansas City	8	8	0
Baltimore	7	9	0	Denver	8	8	0
NY Jets	4	12	0	Seattle	4	12	0
Philadelphia	12	4	0	Atlanta	12	4	0
Dallas	12	4	0	Los Angeles	11	5	0
Washington	6	10	0	San Francisco	6	10	0
St. Louis	5	11	0	New Orleans	1	15	0
NY Giants	4	12	0				

U.S BADMINTON CHAMPIONSHIPS
WINNERS

Mens Singles	Womens Singles	Mens Doubles	Womens Doubles	Mixed Doubles
Gary Higgins	Cheryl Carton	Matt Fogarty Mike Walker	Pam Brady Judianne Kelly	Mike Walker Judianne Kelly

NBA STANDINGS
DIVISION STANDINGS

Team	W	L	W/L%	GB	PS/G	PA/G	SRS
Eastern Division							
Boston Celtics	61	21	.744	–	113.5	105.7	7.37
Philadelphia 76ers	59	23	.720	2.0	109.1	104.9	4.04
Washington Bullets	39	43	.476	22.0	107.0	109.5	-2.27
New York Knicks	39	43	.476	22.0	114.0	115.1	-0.96
New Jersey Nets	34	48	.415	27.0	108.3	109.5	-0.98
Atlanta Hawks	50	32	.610	---	104.5	101.6	2.83
Houston Rockets	41	41	.500	9.0	110.8	110.6	0.27
San Antonio Spurs	41	41	.500	9.0	119.4	119.7	-0.24
Indiana Pacers	37	45	.451	13.0	111.2	111.9	-0.54
Cleveland Cavaliers	37	45	.451	13.0	114.1	113.8	0.43
Detroit Pistons	16	66	.195	34.0	108.9	117.2	-7.57
Western Division							
Milwaukee Bucks	49	33	.598	------	110.1	106.1	3.57
Kansas City Kings	47	35	.573	2.0	108.0	104.9	2.82
Denver Nuggets	30	52	.366	19.0	108.3	112.7	-4.22

Chicago Bulls	30	52	.366	19.0	107.5	110.2	-2.63
Utah Jazz	24	58	.293	25.0	102.4	108.4	-5.71
Los Angeles Lakers	60	22	.732	---	115.1	109.2	5.40
Seattle Supersonics	56	26	.683	4.0	108.5	103.8	4.24
Phoenix Suns	55	27	.671	5.0	111.1	107.5	3.25
Portland Trail Blazers	38	44	.463	22.0	102.5	103.3	-0.87
San Diego Clippers	35	47	.427	25.0	107.6	111.7	-3.97
Golden State Warriors	24	58	.293	36.0	103.6	108.0	-4.20

AMERICAN HORSE OF THE YEAR
ECLIPSE AWARD

Horse	Trainer	Owner	Age	Gender
Spectacular Bid	Bud Delp	Hawksworth Farm	4	C

NHL SEASON
FINAL STANDINGS

Prince of Wale / Clarence Campbell	GP	W	L	T	Pts	GF	GA	PIM
Buffalo Sabres	80	39	20	21	99	327	250	1194
Boston Bruins	80	37	30	13	87	316	272	1836
Minnesota North Stars	80	35	28	17	87	291	263	1624
Quebec Nordiques	80	30	32	18	78	314	318	1524
Toronto Maple Leafs	80	28	37	15	71	322	367	1830
Montreal Canadiens	80	45	22	13	103	332	232	1398
Los Angeles Kings	80	43	24	13	99	337	290	1627
Chicago Black Hawks	80	31	33	16	78	304	315	1660
Pittsburgh Penguins	80	30	37	13	73	302	345	1807
Hartford Whalers	80	21	41	18	60	292	372	1584
Detroit Red Wings	80	19	43	18	56	252	339	1687
New York Islanders	80	48	18	14	110	355	260	1442
Philadelphia Flyers	80	41	24	15	97	313	249	2621
Calgary Flames	80	39	27	14	92	329	298	1450
New York Rangers	80	30	36	14	74	312	317	1981
Washington Capitals	80	26	36	18	70	286	317	1872
St. Louis Blues	80	45	18	17	107	352	281	1657
Vancouver Canucks	80	28	32	20	76	289	301	1892
Edmonton Oilers	80	29	35	16	74	328	327	1544
Colorado Rockies	80	22	45	13	57	258	344	1418
Winnipeg Jets	80	9	57	14	32	246	400	1191

MAJOR LEAGUE BASEBALL SEASON HISTORY

American League Standings

TEAM	W	L	PCT	GB	HOME	ROAD	RS	RA	DIFF
New York	103	59	.636	------	------	------	820	662	+158
Baltimore	100	62	.617	3	---	---	805	640	+165
Milwaukee	86	76	.531	17	---	---	811	682	+129
Boston	83	77	.519	19	---	---	757	767	-10
Detroit	84	78	.515	19	---	---	830	757	+73
Cleveland	79	81	.494	23	---	---	738	807	-69
Toronto	67	95	.414	36	---	---	624	762	-138
Kansas City	97	65	.599	---	---	---	809	694	_115
Oakland	83	79	.512	14	---	---	686	642	+44
Minnesota	77	84	.478	19.5	---	---	670	724	-54
Texas	76	85	.466	20.5	---	---	756	752	+4
Chicago	70	90	.432	26	---	---	587	722	-135
California	65	95	.406	31	---	---	698	797	-99
Seattle	59	103	.362	38	---	---	610	793	-183

National League Standings

TEAM	W	L	PCT	GB	HOME	ROAD	RS	RA	DIFF
Philadelphia	91	71	.562	---	---	---	728	639	+89
Montreal	90	72	.556	1	---	---	694	629	+65
Pittsburgh	83	79	.512	8	000	000	666	646	+20
St. Louis	74	88	.457	17	---	---	738	710	+28
New York	67	95	.414	24	---	---	611	702	-91
Chicago	64	98	.395	27	---	---	614	728	-114
Houston	93	70	.571	---	---	---	637	589	+48
Los Angeles	92	71	.564	1	---	---	663	591	+72
Cincinnati	89	73	.546	3.5	---	---	707	670	+37
Atlanta	81	80	.503	11	---	---	630	660	-30
San Francisco	75	86	.466	17	---	---	573	634	-61
San Diego	73	89	.448	19.5	---	---	591	654	-63

1981

NATIONAL FOOTBALL LEAGUE SEASON STANDINGS

EAST	W	L	T	WEST	W	L	T
Miami	11	4	1	San Diego	10	6	0
NY Jets	10	5	1	Denver	10	6	0
Buffalo	10	6	0	Kansas City	9	7	0
New England	2	14	0	Oakland	7	9	0
Dallas	12	4	0	Seattle	6	10	0
Philadelphia	10	6	0	San Francisco	13	3	0
NY Giants	9	7	0	Atlanta	7	9	0
Washington	8	8	0	Los Angeles	6	10	0
St. Louis	7	9	0	New Orleans	4	12	0

U.S BADMINTON CHAMPIONSHIPS WINNERS

Mens Singles	Womens Singles	Mens Doubles	Womens Doubles	Mixed Doubles
Chris Kinard	Utami Kinard	John Britton Gary Higgins	Pam Brady Judianne Kelly	Danny Brady Pam Brady

NBA STANDINGS DIVISION STANDINGS

Team	W	L	W/L%	GB	PS/G	PA/G	SRS
Eastern Division							
Boston Celtics	62	20	.756	---	109.9	104.0	6.05
Philadelphia 76ers	62	20	.756	---	111.7	103.8	7.76
New York Knicks	50	32	.610	12.0	107.9	106.3	2.00
Washington Bullets	39	43	.476	23.0	105.6	105.6	0.42
New Jersey Nets	24	58	.293	38.0	106.9	113.0	-5.15
Milwaukee Bucks	60	22	.732	---	113.1	105.9	7.14
Chicago Bulls	45	37	.549	15.0	109.0	107.0	2.34
Indiana Pacers	44	38	.537	16.0	107.6	106.2	1.72
Atlanta Hawks	31	51	.378	29.0	104.9	108.0	-2.37
Cleveland Cavaliers	28	54	.341	32.0	105.7	110.6	-4.15
Detroit Pistons	21	61	.256	39.0	99.7	106.0	-5.58
Western Division							
San Antonio Spurs	52	30	.634	------	112.3	109.4	2.18
Kansas City Kings	40	42	.488	12.0	106.9	106.9	-0.49
Houston Rockets	40	42	.488	12.0	108.3	107.9	-0.20
Denver Nuggets	37	45	.451	15.0	121.8	122.3	-0.95

Utah Jazz	28	54	.341	24.0	101.2	107.1	-5.99
Dallas Mavericks	15	67	.183	37.0	101.5	109.9	-8.33
Phoenix Suns	57	25	.695	---	110.0	104.5	4.83
Los Angeles Lakers	54	28	.659	3.0	111.2	107.3	3.27
Portland Trail Blazer	45	37	.549	12.0	110.7	109.8	0.52
Golden State Warriors	39	43	.476	18.0	109.8	111.0	-1.41
San Diego Clippers	36	46	.439	21.0	106.5	108.1	-1.78
Seattle SuperSonics	34	48	.415	23.0	104.0	105.7	-1.84

AMERICAN HORSE OF THE YEAR
ECLIPSE AWARD

Horse	Trainer	Owner	Age	Gender
John Henry	Ron McAnally	Dotsam Stable	6	G

NHL SEASON
FINAL STANDINGS

Prince of Wales / Clarence Campbell	GP	W	L	T	Pts	GF	GA	PIM
Montreal Canadiens	80	46	17	17	109	360	223	1463
Boston Bruins	80	43	27	10	96	323	285	1266
Buffalo Sabres	80	39	26	15	93	307	273	1425
Quebec Nordiques	80	33	31	16	82	356	345	1757
Hartford Whalers	80	21	41	18	60	264	351	1493
New York Islanders	80	54	16	10	118	385	250	1328
New York Rangers	80	39	27	14	92	316	306	1402
Philadelphia Flyers	80	38	31	11	87	325	313	2493
Pittsburgh Penguins	80	31	36	13	75	310	337	2212
Washington Capitals	80	26	41	13	65	319	338	1932
Minnesota North Stars	80	37	23	20	94	346	288	1358
Winnipeg Jets	80	33	33	14	80	319	332	1314
St. Louis Blues	80	32	40	8	72	315	349	1579
Chicago Black Hawks	80	30	38	12	72	332	363	1775
Toronto Maple Leafs	80	20	44	16	56	298	380	1888
Detroit Red Wings	80	21	47	12	54	270	351	1250
Edmonton Oilers	80	48	17	15	111	417	295	1473
Vancouver Canucks	80	30	33	17	77	290	286	1840
Calgary Flames	80	29	34	17	75	334	345	1331
Los Angeles Kings	80	24	41	15	63	314	396	1730
Colorado Rockets	80	18	49	13	49	241	362	1138

MAJOR LEAGUE BASEBALL SEASON HISTORY

American League Standings

TEAM	W	L	PCT	GB	HOME	ROAD	RS	RA	DIFF
Milwaukee	62	47	.569	---	---	---	493	459	+34
Baltimore	59	46	.562	1	---	---	429	437	-8
New York	59	48	.551	2	---	---	421	343	+78
Detroit	60	49	.550	2	---	---	427	404	+23
Boston	59	49	.546	2.5	---	---	519	481	+38
Cleveland	52	51	.505	7	---	---	431	442	-11
Toronto	37	69	.349	23.5	---	---	329	466	-137
Oakland	64	45	.587	---	---	---	458	403	+55
Texas	57	48	.543	5	---	---	452	389	+63
Chicago	54	52	.509	8.5	---	---	476	423	+53
Kansas City	50	53	.485	11	---	---	397	405	-8
California	51	59	.464	13.5	---	---	476	453	+23
Seattle	44	65	.400	20	---	---	426	521	-95
Minnesota	41	68	.373	23	---	---	378	486	-108

National League Standings

TEAM	W	L	PCT	GB	HOME	ROAD	RS	RA	DIFF
St. Louis	59	43	.573	---	---	---	464	417	+47
Montreal	60	48	.556	2	---	---	443	394	+49
Philadelphia	59	48	.551	2.5	---	---	491	472	+19
Pittsburgh	46	56	.447	13	---	---	407	425	-18
New York	41	62	.390	18.5	---	---	348	432	-84
Chicago	38	65	.358	21.5	---	---	370	483	-113
Cincinnati	66	42	.611	---	---	---	464	440	+24
Los Angeles	63	47	.573	4	---	---	450	356	+94
Houston	61	49	.555	6	---	---	394	331	+63
San Francisco	56	55	.505	11.5	---	---	427	414	+13
Atlanta	50	56	.467	15	---	---	395	416	-21
San Diego	41	69	.373	26	---	---	382	455	-73

1982

NATIONAL FOOTBALL LEAGUE SEASON STANDINGS

AFC	W	L	T	NFC	W	L	T
LA Raiders	8	1	0	Washington	8	1	0
Miami	7	2	0	Dallas	6	3	0
Cincinnati	7	2	0	Green Bay	5	3	1
Pittsburgh	6	3	0	Minnesota	5	4	0
San Diego	6	3	0	Atlanta	5	4	0
NY Jets	6	3	0	St. Louis	5	4	0
New England	5	4	0	Tampa Bay	5	4	0
Cleveland	4	5	0	Detroit	4	5	0
Buffalo	4	5	0	NY Giants	4	5	0
Seattle	4	5	0	New Orleans	4	5	0
Kansas City	3	6	0	San Francisco	3	6	0
Denver	2	7	0	Chicago	3	6	0
Houston	1	8	0	Philadelphia	3	6	0
Baltimore	0	8	1	LA Rams	2	7	0

U.S BADMINTON CHAMPIONSHIPS WINNERS

Mens Singles	Womens Singles	Mens Doubles	Womens Doubles	Mixed Doubles
Gary Higgins	Cheryl Carton	Don Paup Bruce Pontow	Pam Brady Judianne Kelly	Danny Brady Pam Brady

NBA STANDINGS DIVISION STANDINGS

Team	W	L	W/L%	GB	PS/G	PA/G	SRS
East							
Boston Celtics	63	19	.768	–	112.0	105.6	6.35
Philadelphia 76ers	58	24	.707	5.0	111.2	105.5	5.74
New Jersey Nets	44	38	.537	19.0	106.7	106.0	0.87
Washington Bullets	43	39	.524	20.0	103.5	102.6	1.06
New York Knicks	33	49	.402	30.0	106.2	108.9	-2.15
Milwaukee Bucks	55	27	.671	---	108.4	102.9	5.38
Atlanta Hawks	42	40	.512	13.0	101.0	100.5	0.81
Detroit Pistons	39	43	.476	16.0	111.1	112.0	-0.63
Indiana Pacers	35	47	.427	20.0	102.2	104.0	-1.49
Chicago Bulls	34	48	.415	21.0	106.6	108.6	-1.57
Cleveland Cavaliers	15	67	.183	40.0	103.2	111.7	-7.77

West

San Antonio Spurs	48	34	.585	---	113.1	110.8	1.79
Denver Nuggets	46	36	.561	2.0	126.5	126.0	0.13
Houston Rockets	46	36	.561	2.0	105.9	105.9	-0.39
Kansas City Kings	30	52	.366	18.0	107.1	110.2	-3.25
Dallas Mavericks	28	54	.341	20.0	104.6	109.0	-4.48
Utah Jazz	25	57	.305	23.0	110.9	116.6	-5.63
Los Angeles Lakers	57	25	.695	---	144.6	109.8	4.37
Seattle SuperSonics	52	30	.634	5.0	107.3	103.1	3.69
Phoenix Suns	46	36	.561	11.0	106.2	102.7	3.05
Golden State Warriors	45	37	.549	12.0	110.9	109.8	0.80
Portland Trail Blazers	42	40	.512	15.0	109.8	109.2	0.39
San Diego Clippers	17	65	.207	40.0	108.5	115.9	-7.05

AMERICAN HORSE OF THE YEAR
ECLIPSE AWARD

Horse	Trainer	Owner	Age	Gender
Conquistador Cielo	Woody Stephens	Henryk de Kwiatkowski	3	C

NHL SEASON
FINAL STANDINGS

Princes of Wales / Clarence Campbell	GP	W	L	T	Pts	GF	GA	PIM
Boston Bruins	80	50	20	10	110	327	228	1202
Montreal Canadiens	80	42	24	14	98	350	286	1116
Buffalo Sabres	80	38	29	13	89	318	285	1031
Quebec Nordiques	80	34	34	12	80	343	336	1648
Hartford Whalers	80	19	54	7	45	261	403	1392
Philadelphia Flyers	80	49	23	8	106	326	240	1337
New York islanders	80	42	26	12	96	302	226	1266
Washington Capitals	80	39	25	16	94	306	283	1329
New York Rangers	80	35	35	10	80	306	287	1100
New Jersey Devils	80	17	49	14	48	230	338	1270
Pittsburgh Penguins	80	18	53	9	45	257	394	1859
Chicago Black Hawks	80	47	23	10	104	338	268	1185
Minnesota North Stars	80	40	24	16	96	321	290	1520
Toronto Maple Leafs	80	28	40	12	68	293	330	1481
St. Louis Blues	80	25	40	15	65	285	316	1281
Detroit Red Wings	80	21	44	15	57	263	344	1064
Edmonton Oilers	80	47	21	12	106	424	315	1771
Calgary Flames	80	32	34	14	78	321	317	1146

1983

NATIONAL FOOTBALL LEAGUE SEASON STANDINGS

EAST	W	L	T	WEST	W	L	T
Miami	12	4	0	LA Raiders	12	4	0
New England	8	8	0	Seattle	9	7	0
Buffalo	8	8	0	Denver	9	7	0
Baltimore	7	9	0	San Diego	6	10	0
NY Jets	7	9	0	Kansas City	6	10	0
Washington	14	2	0	San Francisco	10	6	0
Dallas	12	4	0	LA Ram	9	7	0
St. Louis	8	7	1	New Orleans	8	8	0
Philadelphia	5	11	0	Atlanta	7	9	0
NY Giants	3	12	1				

U.S BADMINTON CHAMPIONSHIPS WINNERS

Mens Singles	Womens Singles	Mens Doubles	Womens Doubles	Mixed Doubles
Rodney Barton	Cheryl Carton	John Britton Gary Higgins	Pam Brady Judianne Kelly	Mike Walker Judianne Kelly

NBA STANDINGS DIVISION STANDINGS

Team	W	L	W/L%	GB	PS/G	PA/G	SRS
East							
Philadelphia 76ers	65	17	.793	-----	112.1	104.4	7.53
Boston Celtics	56	26	.683	9.0	112.1	106.7	5.34
New Jersey Nets	49	33	.598	16.0	105.8	103.0	2.77
New York Knicks	44	38	.537	21.0	100.0	97.5	2.58
Washington Bullets	42	40	.512	23.0	99.2	99.3	0.20
Milwaukee Bucks	51	31	.622	---	106.6	102.2	4.32
Atlanta Hawks	43	39	.524	8.0	101.6	102.6	-0.72
Detroit Pistons	37	45	.451	14.0	112.7	113.1	-0.17
Chicago Bulls	28	54	.341	23.0	111.0	115.9	-4.41
Cleveland Cavaliers	23	59	.280	28.0	97.1	104.6	-6.78
Indiana Pacers	20	62	.244	31.0	108.7	114.5	-5.36
West							
San Antonio Spurs	53	29	.646	---	114.3	110.7	3.10
Denver Nuggets	45	37	.549	8.0	123.2	122.6	0.27
Kansas City Kings	45	37	.549	8.0	113.8	112.3	1.04

Dallas Mavericks	38	44	.463	15.0	112.7	113.1	-0.70
Utah Jazz	30	52	.366	23.0	109.0	113.2	-4.22
Houston Rockets	14	68	.171	39.0	99.3	110.9	-11.1
Los Angeles Lakers	58	24	.707	---	115.0	109.5	5.06
Phoenix Suns	53	29	.646	5.0	107.0	102.0	4.61
Seattle SuperSonics	48	34	.585	10.0	110.0	106.8	2.88
Portland Trail Blazers	46	36	.561	12.0	107.4	105.3	1.88
Golden State Warriors	30	52	.366	28.0	108.6	112.3	-3.48
San Diego Clippers	25	57	.305	33.0	108.6	113.4	-4.61

AMERICAN HORSE OF THE YEAR
ECLIPSE AWARD

Horse	Trainer	Owner	Age	Gender
All Along	Patrick Biancone	Daniel Wildenstein	4	F

NHL SEASON
FINAL STANDINGS

Prince of Wales / Clarence Campbell	GP	W	L	T	Pts	GF	GA	PIM
Boston Bruins	80	49	25	6	104	336	261	1606
Buffalo Sabres	80	48	25	7	103	315	257	1190
Quebec Nordiques	80	42	28	10	94	360	278	1600
Montreal Canadiens	80	35	40	5	75	286	295	1371
Hartford Whalers	80	28	42	10	66	288	320	1184
New York Islanders	80	50	26	4	104	357	269	1157
Washington Capitals	80	48	27	5	101	308	226	1252
Philadelphia Flyers	80	44	26	10	98	350	290	1488
New York Rangers	80	42	29	9	93	314	304	1471
New Jersey Devils	80	17	56	7	41	231	350	1352
Pittsburgh Penguins	80	16	58	6	38	254	390	1695
Minnesota North Stars	80	39	31	10	88	345	344	1696
St. Louis Blues	80	32	41	7	71	293	316	1614
Detroit Red Wings	80	31	42	7	69	298	323	1546
Chicago Black Hawks	80	30	42	8	68	277	311	1358
Toronto Maple Leafs	80	26	45	9	61	303	387	1682
Edmonton Oilers	80	57	18	5	119	446	314	1577
Calgary Flames	80	34	32	14	82	311	314	1390
Vancouver Canucks	80	32	39	9	73	306	328	1474
Winnipeg Jets	80	31	38	11	73	340	374	1579
Los Angeles Kings	80	23	44	13	59	309	376	1265

MAJOR LEAGUE BASEBALL SEASON HISTORY

American League Standings

TEAM	W	L	PCT	GB	HOME	ROAD	RS	RA	DIFF
Baltimore	98	64	.605	---	---	---	799	652	+147
Detroit	92	70	.568	6	---	---	789	679	+110
New York	91	71	.562	7	---	---	770	703	+67
Toronto	89	73	.549	9	---	---	795	726	+69
Milhawkee	87	75	.537	11	---	---	764	708	+56
Boston	78	84	.481	20	---	---	724	775	-51
Cleveland	70	92	.432	28	---	---	704	785	-81
Chicago	99	63	.611	---	---	---	800	650	+150
Kansas City	79	83	.485	20	---	---	696	767	-71
Texas	77	85	.472	22	---	---	639	609	+30
Oakland	74	88	.457	25	---	---	708	782	-74
California	70	92	.432	29	---	---	722	779	-57
Minnesota	70	92	.432	29	---	---	709	822	-113
Seattle	60	102	.370	39	---	---	558	740	-182

National League Standings

TEAM	W	L	PCT	GB	HOME	ROAD	RS	RA	DIFF
Philadelphia	90	72	.552	---	---	---	696	635	+61
Pittsburgh	84	78	.519	6	---	---	659	648	+11
Montreal	82	80	.503	8	---	---	677	646	+31
St. Louis	79	83	.488	11	---	---	679	710	-31
Chicago	71	91	.438	19	---	---	701	719	-18
New York	68	94	.420	22	---	---	575	680	-105
Los Angeles	91	71	.558	---	---	---	654	609	+45
Atlanta	88	74	.543	3	---	---	746	640	+106
Houston	85	77	.525	6	---	---	643	646	-3
San Diego	81	81	.497	10	---	---	653	653	0
San Francisco	79	83	.488	12	---	---	687	697	-10
Cincinnati	74	88	.457	17	---	---	623	710	-87

U.S NATIONAL TENNIS CHAMPIONSHIPS

Mens Singles – Jimmy Connors defeated Ivan Lendl
Womens Singles – Martina Navratilova defeated Chris Evert
Mens Doubles – Peter Fleming / John McEnroe defeated Fritz Buehning / Van Winitsky
Womens Doubles – Martina Navratilova / Pam Shriver defeated Rosalyn Fairbank / Candy Reynolds
Mixed Doubles – Elizabeth Sayers / John Fitzgerald defeated Barbara Potter / Ferdi Taygan

1984

NATIONAL FOOTBALL LEAGUE SEASON STANDINGS

EAST	W	L	T	WEST	W	L	T
Miami	14	2	0	Denver	13	3	0
New England	9	7	0	Seattle	12	4	0
NY Jets	7	9	0	LA Raiders	11	5	0
Indianapolis	4	12	0	Kansas City	8	8	0
Buffalo	2	14	0	San Diego	7	9	0
Washington	11	5	0	San Francisco	15	1	0
NY Giants	9	7	0	LA Rams	10	6	0
St. Louis	9	7	0	New Orleans	7	9	0
Dallas	9	7	0	Atlanta	4	12	0
Philadelphia	6	9	1				

NBA STANDINGS
DIVISION STANDINGS

Team	W	L	W/L%	GB	PS/G	PA/G	SRS
East							
Boston Celtics	62	20	.756	–	112.1	105.6	6.42
Philadelphia 76ers	52	30	.634	10.0	107.8	105.6	2.39
New York Knicks	47	35	.573	15.0	106.9	103.0	3.79
New Jersey Nets	45	37	.549	17.0	110.0	108.9	1.27
Washington Bullets	35	47	.427	27.0	102.7	105.6	-2.36
Milwaukee Bucks	50	32	.610	---	105.7	101.5	4.04
Detroit Pistons	49	33	.598	1.0	117.1	113.5	3.52
Atlanta Hawks	40	42	.488	10.0	101.5	102.8	-1.08
Cleveland Cavaliers	28	54	.341	22.0	102.3	106.5	-3.71
Chicago Bulls	27	55	.329	23.0	103.7	108.9	-4.69
Indiana Pacers	26	56	.317	24.0	104.5	109.3	-4.25
West							
Utah Jazz	45	37	.549	------	115.0	113.8	0.81
Dallas Mavericks	43	39	.524	2.0	110.4	110.0	0.15
Denver Nuggets	38	44	.463	7.0	123.7	124.8	-1.27
Kansas City Kings	38	44	.463	7.0	110.0	111.5	-1.62
San Antonio Spurs	37	45	.451	8.0	120.3	120.5	-0.50
Houston Rockets	29	53	.354	16.0	110.6	113.7	-3.12
Los Angeles Lakers	54	28	.659	---	115.6	111.8	3.32

Portland Trail Blazers	48	34	.585	6.0	113.1	109.6	3.13
Seattle SuperSonics	42	40	.512	12.0	108.1	108.3	-0.34
Phoenix Suns	41	41	.500	13.0	111.0	110.1	0.65
Golden State Warriors	37	45	.451	17.0	109.9	113.3	-3.35
San Diego Clippers	30	52	.366	24.0	110.7	114.0	-3.21

NHL SEASON
FINAL STANDINGS

Prince of Wales / Clarence Campbell	GP	W	L	T	Pts	GF	GA	PIM
Montreal Canadiens	80	41	27	12	94	309	262	1464
Quebec Nordique	80	41	30	9	91	323	275	1643
Buffalo Sabres	80	38	28	14	90	290	237	1221
Boston Bruins	80	36	34	10	82	303	287	1825
Hartford Whalers	80	30	41	9	69	268	318	1606
Philadelphia Flyers	80	53	20	7	113	348	241	1540
Washington Capitals	80	46	25	9	101	322	240	1161
New York Islanders	80	40	34	6	86	345	312	1516
New York Rangers	80	26	44	10	62	295	345	1301
New Jersey Devils	80	22	48	10	54	264	346	1282
Pittsburgh Penguins	80	24	51	5	53	276	385	1493
St. Louis Blues	80	37	31	12	86	299	288	1301
Chicago Black Hawks	80	38	35	7	83	309	299	1432
Detroit Red Wings	80	27	41	12	66	313	357	1741
Minnesota North Stars	80	25	43	12	62	268	321	1735
Toronto Maple Leafs	80	20	52	8	48	253	358	1627
Edmonton Oilers	80	49	20	11	109	401	298	1567
Winnipeg Jets	80	43	27	10	96	358	332	1540
Calgary Flames	80	41	27	12	94	363	302	1400
Los Angeles Kings	80	34	32	14	82	339	326	1413
Vancouver Canucks	80	25	46	9	59	284	401	1451

U.S BADMINTON CHAMPIONSHIPS
WINNERS

Mens Singles	Womens Singles	Mens Doubles	Womens Doubles	Mixed Doubles
Rodney Barton	Cheryl Carton	Matt Fogarty Bruce Pontow	Pam Brady Monica Ortez	John Britton Cheryl Carton

AMERICAN HORSE OF THE YEAR
ECLIPSE AWARD

Horse	Trainer	Owner	Age	Gender
John Henry	Ron McAnally	Dotsam Stable	9	G

1985

NATIONAL FOOTBALL LEAGUE SEASON STANDINGS

EAST	W	L	T	WEST	W	L	T
Miami	12	4	0	LA Raider	12	4	0
NY Jets	11	5	0	Denver	11	5	0
New England	11	5	0	Seattle	8	8	0
Indianapolis	5	11	0	San Diego	8	8	0
Buffalo	2	14	0	Kansas City	6	10	0
Dallas	10	6	0	LA Rams	11	5	0
NY Giant	10	6	0	San Francisco	10	6	0
Washington	10	6	0	New Orleans	5	11	0
Philadelphia	7	9	0	Atlanta	4	12	0

U.S BADMINTON CHAMPIONSHIPS WINNERS

Mens Singles	Womens Singles	Mens Doubles	Womens Doubles	Mixed Doubles
Chris Jogis	Judianne Kelly	John Britton Gary Higgin	Pam Brady Judianne Kelly	Mike Walker Judianne Kelly

NBA STANDINGS DIVISION STANDINGS

Team	W	L	W/L%	GB	PS/G	PA/G	SRS
East							
Boston Celtics	63	19	.768	–	114.8	108.1	6.47
Philadelphia 76ers	58	24	.707	5.0	112.9	108.8	4.17
New Jersey Nets	42	40	.512	21.0	109.5	109.2	0.64
Washington Bullets	40	42	.488	23.0	105.5	105.8	0.15
New York Knicks	24	58	.293	39.0	105.2	109.8	-4.09
Milwaukee Bucks	59	23	.720	---	110.9	104.0	6.69
Detroit Pistons	46	36	.561	13.0	116.0	113.5	2.73
Chicago Bulls	38	44	.463	21.0	108.7	109.6	-0.50
Cleveland Cavaliers	36	46	.439	23.0	108.6	111.3	-2.27
Atlanta Hawks	34	48	.415	25.0	106.6	108.1	-1.14
Indiana Pacers	22	60	.268	37.0	108.3	114.5	-5.46
West							
Denver Nuggets	52	30	.634	---	120.0	117.6	2.05
Houston Rockets	48	34	.585	4.0	111.2	109.5	1.38
Dallas Mavericks	44	38	.537	8.0	111.2	109.0	1.80
Utah Jazz	41	41	.500	11.0	109.0	109.1	-0.33

San Antonio Spurs	41	41	.500	11.0	114.8	113.9	0.63
Kansas City Kings	31	51	.378	21.0	114.8	117.8	-2.71
Los Angeles Lakers	62	20	.756	---	118.2	110.9	6.48
Portland Trail Blazers	42	40	.512	20.0	115.5	112.1	2.80
Phoenix Suns	36	46	.439	26.0	108.0	110.1	-2.34
Seattle SuperSonics	31	51	.378	31.0	102.1	107.6	-5.44
Los Angeles Clippers	31	51	.378	31.0	107.1	111.6	-4.55
Golden State Warriors	22	60	.268	40.0	110.4	117.7	-7.21

AMERICAN HORSE OF THE YEAR
ECLIPSE AWARD

Horse	Trainer	Owner	Age	Gender
Spend A Buck	Cam Gambolati	Hunter Farm	3	C

NHL SEASON
FINAL STANDINGS

Price of Wales / Clarence Campbell	GP	W	L	T	Pts	GF	GA	PIM
Quebec Nordiques	80	43	31	6	92	330	289	1847
Montreal Canadiens	80	40	33	7	87	330	280	1372
Boston Bruins	80	37	31	12	86	311	288	1919
Hartford Whalers	80	40	36	4	84	332	302	1759
Buffalo Sabres	80	37	37	6	80	296	291	1608
Philadelphia Flyers	80	53	23	4	110	335	241	2025
Washington Capitals	80	50	23	7	107	315	272	1418
New York Islanders	80	39	29	12	90	327	284	1343
New York Rangers	80	36	38	6	78	280	276	1496
Pittsburgh Penguins	80	34	38	8	76	313	305	1538
New Jersey Devils	80	28	49	3	59	300	374	1424
Chicago Black Hawks	80	39	33	8	86	351	349	1537
Minnesota North Stars	80	38	33	9	85	327	305	1672
St. Louis Blues	80	37	34	9	83	302	291	1478
Toronto Maple Leafs	80	25	48	7	57	311	386	1716
Detroit Red Wings	80	17	57	6	40	266	415	2393
Edmonton Oilers	80	56	17	7	119	426	310	1928
Calgary Flames	80	40	31	9	89	354	315	2297
Winnipeg Jets	80	26	47	7	59	295	372	1774
Vancouver Canucks	80	23	44	13	59	282	333	1813
Los Angeles Kings	80	23	49	8	54	284	389	2004

MAJOR LEAGUE BASEBALL SEASON HISTORY

American League Standings

TEAM	W	L	PCT	GB	HOME	ROAD	RS	RA	DIFF
Toronto	99	62	.615	---	---	---	759	588	+171
New York	97	64	.602	2	------	------	839	660	+179
Detroit	84	77	.522	15	---	---	729	688	+41
Baltimore	83	78	.516	16	---	---	818	764	+54
Boston	81	81	.497	18.5	---	---	800	720	+80
Milwaukee	71	90	.441	28	---	---	690	802	-112
Cleveland	60	102	.370	39.5	---	---	729	861	-132
Kansas City	91	71	.562	---	---	---	687	639	+48
California	90	72	.556	1	---	---	732	703	+29
Chicago	85	77	.521	6	---	---	736	720	+16
Minnesota	77	85	.475	14	---	---	705	782	-77
Oakland	77	85	.475	14	---	---	757	787	-39
Seattle	74	88	.457	17	---	---	719	818	-99
Texas	62	99	.385	28.5	---	---	617	785	-168

National League Standings

TEAM	W	L	PCT	GB	HOME	ROAD	RS	RA	DIFF
St. Louis	101	61	.623	---	---	---	747	572	+175
New York	98	64	.605	3	---	---	695	568	+127
Montreal	84	77	.522	16.5	---	---	633	636	-3
Chicago	77	84	475	23.5	---	---	686	729	-43
Philadelphia	75	87	.463	26	---	---	667	673	-6
Pittsburgh	57	104	.354	43.5	---	---	568	708	-140
Los Angeles	95	67	.586	---	---	---	682	579	+103
Cincinnati	89	72	.549	5.5	---	---	677	666	+11
San Diego	83	79	.512	12	---	---	650	622	+28
Houston	83	79	.512	12	---	---	706	691	+15
Atlanta	66	96	.407	29	---	---	632	781	-149
San Francisco	62	100	.383	33	---	---	556	674	-118

U.S NATIONAL TENNIS CHAMPIONSHIPS

Mens Singles – Ivan Lendl defeated John McEnroe
Womens Singles – Hana Mandlikova defeated Martina Navaratilova
Mens Doubles – Ken Flach / Robert Seguso defeated Henri Leconte / Yannick Noah
Womens Doubles – Claudia Kohde-Kilsch / Helena Sukova defeated Martina Navratilova / Pam Shriver
Mixed Doubles – Martina Navratilova / Heinz Gunthardt defeated Elizabeth Smylie / John Fitzgerald

82

1986

NATIONAL FOOTBALL LEAGUE SEASON
STANDINGS

EAST	W	L	T	WEST	W	L	T
New England	11	5	0	Denver	11	5	0
NY Jets	10	6	0	Kansas City	10	6	0
Miami	8	8	0	Seattle	10	6	0
Buffalo	4	12	0	LA Raiders	8	8	0
Indianapolis	3	13	0	San Diego	4	12	0
NY Giants	14	2	0	San Francisco	10	5	1
Washington	12	4	0	LA Rams	10	6	0
Dallas	7	9	0	Atlanta	7	8	1
Philadelphia	5	10	1	New Orleans	7	9	0

U.S BADMINTON CHAMPIONSHIPS
WINNERS

Mens Singles	Womens Singles	Mens Doubles	Womens Doubles	Mixed Doubles
Chris Jogis	Nina Lolk	Matt Fogarty Bruce Pontow	Linda French Nina Lolk	Mike Walker Judianne Kelly

NBA STANDINGS
DIVISION STANDINGS

Team	W	L	W/L%	GB	PS/G	PA/G	SRS
East							
Boston Celtics	67	15	.817	–	114.1	104.7	9.06
Milwaukee	57	25	.695	---	114.5	105.5	8.69
Philadelphia 76ers	54	28	.659	13.0	110.4	108.0	2.46
Atlanta Hawks	50	32	.610	7.0	108.6	106.2	2.59
Detroit Piston	46	36	.561	11.0	114.2	113.0	1.44
Washington Bullets	39	43	.476	28.0	103.0	104.8	-1.28
New Jersey Nets	39	43	.476	28.0	109.1	111.1	-1.39
Chicago Bulls	30	52	.366	27.0	109.3	113.1	-3.12
Cleveland Cavaliers	29	53	.354	28.0	107.8	110.6	-2.19
Indiana Pacers	26	56	.317	31.0	103.9	107.2	-2.66
New York Knicks	23	59	.280	44.0	98.7	104.3	-4.82
West							
Houston Rockets	51	31	.622	---	114.4	111.8	2.10
Denver Nuggets	47	35	.573	4.0	114.8	113.5	0.89
Dallas Mavericks	44	38	.537	7.0	115.3	114.2	0.70
Utah Jazz	42	40	.512	9.0	108.2	108.5	-0.67

Sacremento Kings	37	45	.451	14.0	108.8	111.9	-3.19
San Antonio Spurs	35	47	.427	16.0	111.2	113.1	-2.06
Los Angeles Lakers	62	20	.756	---	117.3	109.5	6.84
Portland Trail Blazers	40	42	.488	22.0	115.1	114.0	0.61
Phoenix Suns	32	50	.390	30.0	110.0	113.0	-3.16
Los Angeles Clippers	32	50	.390	30.0	108.6	115.5	-6.83

NHL SEASON
FINAL STANDINGS

Prince of Wales / Clarence Campbell	GP	W	L	T	Pts	GF	GA	PIM
Hartford Whalers	80	43	30	7	93	287	270	1496
Montreal Canadiens	80	41	29	10	92	277	241	1802
Boston Bruins	80	39	34	7	85	301	276	1870
Quebec Nordiques	80	31	39	10	72	267	267	1741
Buffalo Sabres	80	28	44	8	64	280	308	1810
Philadelphia Flyers	80	46	26	8	100	310	245	2082
Washington Capitals	80	38	32	10	86	285	278	1720
New York Islanders	80	35	33	12	82	279	281	1857
New York Rangers	80	34	38	8	76	307	323	1718
Pittsburgh Penguins	80	30	38	12	72	297	290	1693
New Jersey Devils	80	29	45	6	64	293	368	1735
St. Louis Blues	80	32	33	15	79	281	293	1572
Detroit Red Wings	80	34	36	10	78	260	274	2209
Chicago Black Hawks	80	29	37	14	72	290	310	1692
Toronto Maple Leafs	80	32	42	6	70	286	319	1827
Minnesota North Stars	80	30	40	10	70	296	314	1936
Edmonton Oilers	80	50	24	6	106	372	284	1721
Calgary Flames	80	46	31	3	95	318	289	2036
Winnipeg Jets	80	40	32	8	88	279	271	1537

AMERICAN HORSE OF THE YEAR
ECLIPSE AWARD

Horse	Trainer	Owner	Age	Gender
Lady's Secret	D. Wayne Lukas	Eugene V. Klein	4	F

84

1987

NATIONAL FOOTBALL LEAGUE SEASON
STANDINGS

EAST	W	L	T	WEST	W	L	T
Indianapolis	9	6	0	Denver	10	4	1
New England	8	7	0	Seattle	9	6	0
Miami	8	7	0	San Diego	8	7	0
Buffalo	7	8	0	LA Raiders	5	10	0
NY Jets	6	9	0	Kansas City	4	11	0
Washington	11	4	0	San Francisco	13	2	0
Dallas	7	8	0	New Orleans	12	3	0
St. Louis	7	8	0	LA Rams	6	9	0
Philadelphia	7	8	0	Atlanta	3	12	0
NY Giants	6	9	0				

U.S BADMINTON CHAMPIONSHIPS
WINNERS

Mens Singles	Womens Singles	Mens Doubles	Womens Doubles	Mixed Doubles
Tariq Woods	Joy Kitzmiller	Chris Jogis Benny Lee	Linda French Nina Loolk	Chris Jogis Linda French

NBA STANDINGS
DIVISION STANDINGS

Team	W	L	W/L%	GB	PS/G	PA/G	SRS
East							
Boston Celtics	59	23	.720	–	112.6	106.0	6.57
Philadelphia 76ers	45	37	.549	14.0	106.5	106.6	0.11
Washington Bullets	42	40	.512	17.0	106.0	107.3	-1.02
New Jersey Nets	24	58	.293	35.0	108.5	113.5	-4.42
New York Knicks	24	58	.293	35.0	103.8	110.0	-5.42
Atlanta Hawks	57	25	.695	---	110.0	102.8	7.18
Detroit Pistons	52	30	.634	5.0	111.2	107.8	3.51
Milwaukee Bucks	50	32	.610	7.0	110.4	106.5	4.04
Indiana Pacers	41	41	.500	16.0	106.1	106.7	-0.17
Chicago Bulls	40	42	.488	17.0	104.8	103.9	1.26
Cleveland Cavaliers	31	51	.378	26.0	104.4	108.2	-3.19
West							
Dallas Mavericks	55	27	.671	---	116.7	110.4	5.54
Utah Jazz	44	38	.537	11.0	107.9	107.5	0.04
Houston Rockets	42	40	.512	13.0	106.9	105.9	0.60

Denver Nuggets	37	45	.451	18.0	116.7	117.6	-1.14
Sacramento Kings	29	53	.354	26.0	110.9	114.1	-3.34
San Antonio Spurs	28	54	.341	27.0	108.3	113.4	-5.09
Los Angeles Lakers	65	17	.793	---	117.8	108.5	8.32
Portland Trail Blazers	49	33	.598	16.0	117.9	114.8	2.57
Golden State Warriors	42	40	.512	23.0	112.0	114.4	-2.54
Seattle SuperSonics	39	43	.476	26.0	113.7	113.3	0.08
Phoenix Suns	36	46	.439	29.0	111.1	113.5	-2.63
Los Angeles Clippers	12	70	.146	53.0	104.5	115.9	-11.00

AMERICAN HORSE OF THE YEAR
ECLIPSE AWARD

Horse	Trainer	Owner	Age	Gender
Ferdinand	Charlie Whittingham	Elizabeth A. Keck	4	C

NHL SEASON
FINAL STANDINGS

Prince of Wales / Clarence Campbell	GP	W	L	T	Pts	GF	GA	PIM
Montreal Canadiens	80	45	22	13	103	298	238	1830
Boston Bruins	80	44	30	6	94	300	251	2443
Buffalo Sabres	80	37	32	11	85	283	305	2277
Hartford Whalers	80	35	38	7	77	249	267	2046
Quebec Nordiques	80	32	43	5	69	271	306	2042
New York Islanders	80	39	31	10	88	308	267	1732
Philadelphia Flyers	80	38	33	9	85	292	292	2194
Washington Capitals	80	38	33	9	85	281	249	1680
New Jersey Devils	80	38	36	6	82	295	296	2315
New York Rangers	80	36	34	10	82	300	283	1775
Pittsburgh Penguins	80	36	35	9	81	319	316	2211
Detroit Red Wings	80	41	28	11	93	322	269	2391
St. Louis Blues	80	34	38	8	76	278	294	1919
Chicago Black Hawks	80	30	41	9	69	284	328	2228
Toronto Maple Leafs	80	21	49	10	52	273	345	1782
Minnesota North Stars	80	19	48	13	51	242	349	2313
Calgary Flames	80	48	23	9	105	397	305	2431
Edmonton Oilers	80	44	25	11	99	363	288	2173
Winnipeg Jets	80	33	36	11	77	292	310	2278
Los Angeles Kings	80	30	42	8	68	318	359	2124
Vancouver Canucks	80	25	46	9	59	272	320	2196

1988

NATIONAL FOOTBALL LEAGUE SEASON STANDINGS

EAST	W	L	T	WEST	W	L	T
Buffalo	12	4	0	Seattle	9	7	0
Indianapolis	9	7	0	Denver	8	8	0
New England	9	7	0	LA Raider	7	9	0
NY Jets	8	7	1	San Diego	6	10	0
Miami	6	10	0	Kansas City	4	10	0
Philadelphia	10	6	0	San Francisco	10	6	0
NY Giants	10	6	0	LA Rams	10	6	0
Washington	7	9	0	New Orleans	10	6	0
Phoenix	7	9	0	Atlanta	5	11	0
Dallas	3	13	0				

U.S BADMINTON CHAMPIONSHIPS WINNERS

Mens Singles	Womens Singles	Mens Doubles	Womens Doubles	Mixed Doubles
Chris Jogis	Joy Kitzmiller	Chris Jogis Benny Lee	Linda French Linda Safarik-Tong	Chris Jogis Linda French

NBA STANDINGS DIVISION STANDINGS

Team	W	L	W/L%	GB	PS/G	PA/G	SRS
East							
Boston Celtics	57	25	.695	--	113.6	107.7	6.15
Washington Bullets	38	44	.463	19.0	105.5	106.3	-0.16
New York Knicks	38	44	.463	19.0	105.5	106.0	0.14
Philadelphia 76ers	36	46	.439	21.0	105.7	107.1	-0.79
New Jersey Nets	19	63	.232	38.0	100.4	108.5	-6.98
Detroit Pistons	54	28	.659	---	109.2	104.1	5.46
Chicago Bulls	50	32	.610	4.0	105.0	101.6	3.76
Atlanta Hawks	50	32	.610	4.0	107.9	104.3	4.02
Milwaukee Bucks	42	40	.512	12.0	106.1	105.5	1.21
Cleveland Cavaliers	42	40	.512	12.0	104.5	103.7	1.28
Indiana Pacers	38	44	.463	16.0	104.6	105.4	-0.18
West							
Denver Nuggets	54	28	.659	------	116.7	112.7	3.32
Dallas Mavericks	53	29	.646	1.0	109.3	104.9	3.59
Utah Jazz	47	35	.573	7.0	108.5	104.8	2.96

Houston Rockets	46	36	.561	8.0	109.0	107.6	0.82
San Antonio Spurs	31	51	.378	23.0	113.6	118.5	-5.02
Sacremento Kings	24	58	.293	30.0	108.0	113.7	-5.84
Los Angeles Lakers	62	20	.756	---	122.8	107.0	4.81
Portland Trail Blazers	53	29	.646	9.0	116.1	111.5	3.59
Seattle SuperSonics	44	38	.537	18.0	111.4	109.3	1.29
Phoenix Suns	28	54	.341	34.0	108.5	113.0	-4.80
Golden State Warriors	20	62	.244	42.0	107.0	115.3	-8.38
Los Angeles Clippers	17	65	.207	45.0	98.8	109.1	-10.24

AMERICAN HORSE OF THE YEAR
ECLIPSE AWARD

Horse	Trainer	Owner	Age	Gender
Alysheba	Jack Van Berg	Dorothy & Pamela Scharbauer	4	C

NHL SEASON
FINAL STANDINGS

Princes of Wales / Clarence Campbell	GP	W	L	T	Pts	GF	GA	PIM
Montreal Canadiens	80	53	18	9	115	315	218	1537
Boston Bruins	80	37	29	14	88	289	256	1929
Buffalo Sabres	80	38	35	7	83	291	299	2034
Hartford Whalers	80	37	38	5	79	299	290	1672
Quebec Nordiques	80	27	46	7	61	269	342	2004
Washington Capitals	80	41	29	10	92	305	259	1836
Pittsburgh Penguins	80	40	33	7	87	347	349	2670
New York Rangers	80	37	35	8	82	310	307	1891
Philadelphia Flyers	80	36	36	8	80	307	285	2317
New Jersey Devils	80	27	41	12	66	281	325	2499
New York Islanders	80	28	47	5	61	265	325	1822
Detroit Red Wings	80	34	34	12	80	313	316	2245
St. Louis Blues	80	33	35	12	78	275	285	1675
Minnesota North Stars	80	27	37	16	70	258	278	1972
Chicago Black Hawks	80	27	41	12	66	297	35	2496
Toronto Maple Leafs	80	28	46	6	62	259	342	1740
Calgary Flames	80	54	17	9	117	354	226	2444
Los Angeles Kings	80	42	31	7	91	376	335	2215
Edmonton Oilers	80	38	34	8	84	325	306	1931
Vancouver Canucks	80	33	39	8	74	251	253	1569
Winnipeg Jets	80	26	42	12	64	300	355	1843

MAJOR LEAGUE BASEBALL SEASON HISTORY

American League Standings

TEAM	W	L	PCT	GB	HOME	ROAD	RS	RA	DIFF
Boston	89	73	.549	---	---	---	813	689	+124
Detroit	88	74	.543	1	------	------	703	658	+45
Toronto	87	75	.537	2	---	---	763	680	+83
Milwaukee	87	75	.537	2	---	---	682	616	+66
New York	85	76	.528	3.5	---	---	772	748	+24
Cleveland	78	84	.481	11	---	---	666	731	-65
Baltimore	54	107	.335	34.5	---	---	550	789	-239
Oakland	104	58	.642	---	---	---	800	620	+180
Minnesota	91	71	.562	13	---	---	759	672	+87
Kansas	84	77	.522	19.5	---	---	704	648	+56
California	75	87	.463	29	---	---	714	771	-57
Chicago	71	90	.441	32.5	---	---	631	757	-126
Texas	70	91	.435	33.5	---	---	637	735	-98
Seattle	68	93	.422	35.5	---	---	664	744	-80

National League Standings

TEAM	W	L	PCT	GB	HOME	ROAD	RS	RA	DIFF
New York	100	60	.625	---	---	---	703	532	+171
Pittsburgh	85	75	.531	15	---	---	651	616	+35
Montreal	81	81	.497	20	---	---	628	592	+36
Chicago	77	85	.472	24	---	---	660	694	-34
St. Louis	76	86	.469	25	---	---	578	633	-55
Philadelphia	65	96	.401	35.5	---	---	597	734	-137
Los Angeles	94	67	.580	---	---	---	628	544	+84
Cincinnati	87	74	.540	7	---	---	641	596	+45
San Diego	83	78	.516	11	---	---	594	583	+11
San Francisco	83	79	.512	11.5	---	---	670	626	+44
Houston	82	80	.506	12.5	---	---	617	631	-14
Atlanta	54	106	.338	39.5	---	---	555	741	-186

U.S NATIONAL TENNIS CHAMPIONSHIPS

Mens Singles – Mats Wilander defeated Ivan Lendl
Womens Singles – Steffi Graf defeated Gabriela Sabatini
Mens Doubles – Sergioi Casal / Emilio Sanchez defeated Rick Leach / Jim Pugh
Womens Doubles – Gigi Fernandez / Robin White defeated Patty Fendick / Jill Hetheringtono
Mixed Doubles – Jana Novotna / Jim Pugh defeated Elizabeth Smylie / Patrick McEnroe

89

1989

NATIONAL FOOTBALL LEAGUE SEASON STANDINGS

EAST	W	L	T	WEST	W	L	T
Buffalo	9	7	0	Denver	11	5	0
Indianapolis	8	8	0	Kansas City	8	7	1
Miami	8	8	0	LA Raiders	8	8	0
New England	5	11	0	Seattle	7	9	0
NY Jets	4	12	0	San Diego	6	10	0
NY Giants	12	4	0	San Francisco	14	2	0
Philadelphia	11	5	0	LA Rams	11	5	0
Washington	10	6	0	New Orleans	9	7	0
Phoenix	5	11	0	Atlanta	3	13	0
Dallas	1	15	0				

U.S BADMINTON CHAMPIONSHIPS WINNERS

Mens Singles	Womens Singles	Mens Doubles	Womens Doubles	Mixed Doubles
Tariq Wadood	Linda Safarik-Tong	Chris Jogis Benny Lee	Linda French Linda Safarik-Tong	Tariq Wadood Linda French

NBA STANDINGS DIVISION STANDINGS

Team	W	L	W/L%	GB	PS/G	PA/G	SRS
East							
New York Knicks	52	30	.634	–	116.7	112.9	3.62
Philadelphia 76ers	46	36	.561	6.0	111.9	110.4	1.68
Boston Celtics	42	40	.512	10.0	109.2	108.1	1.26
Washington Bullets	40	42	.488	12.0	108.3	110.4	-1.77
New Jersey Nets	26	56	.317	26.0	103.7	110.1	-5.69
Charlotte Hornets	20	62	.244	32.0	104.5	113.0	-7.74
Detroit Pistons	63	19	.768	---	106.6	100.8	6.24
Cleveland Cavaliers	57	255	.695	6.0	108.8	101.2	7.95
Atlanta Hawks	52	30	.634	11.0	111.0	106.1	5.26
Milwaukee Bucks	49	33	.598	14.0	108.9	105.3	4.11
Chicago Bulls	47	35	.573	16.0	106.4	105.0	2.13
Indiana Pacers	28	54	.341	35.0	106.9	111.1	-3.00
West							
Utah Jazz	51	31	.622	---	104.7	99.7	4.01
Houston Rockets	45	37	.549	6.0	108.5	107.5	0.22

Denver Nuggets	44	38	.537	7.0	118.0	116.3	0.91
Dallas Mavericks	38	44	.463	13.0	103.5	104.7	-1.79
San Antonio Spurs	21	61	.256	30.0	105.5	112.8	-7.45
Miami Heat	15	67	.183	36.0	97.8	109.0	-11.13
Los Angeles Lakers	57	25	.695	---	114.7	107.5	6.38
Phoenix Suns	55	27	.671	2.0	118.6	110.9	6.84
Seattle SuperSonics	47	35	.573	10.0	112.1	109.2	2.44
Golden State Warriors	43	39	.524	14.0	116.6	16.9	-0.59
Portland Trail Blazers	39	43	.476	18.0	114.6	113.1	0.92
Sacramento Kings	27	55	.329	30.0	105.5	111.0	-5.35
Los Angeles Clippers	21	61	.256	36.0	106.2	116.2	-9.50

NHL SEASON
FINAL STANDINGS

Princes of Wales / Clarence Campbell	GP	W	L	T	Pts	GF	GA	PIM
Boston Bruins	80	46	25	9	101	289	232	1458
Buffalo Sabres	80	45	27	8	98	286	248	1449
Montreal Canadiens	80	41	28	11	93	288	234	1590
Hartford Whalers	80	38	33	9	85	275	268	2102
Quebec Nordiques	80	12	61	7	31	240	407	2104
New York Rangers	80	36	31	13	85	279	267	2021
New Jersey Devils	80	37	34	9	83	295	288	1659
Washington Capitals	80	36	38	6	78	284	275	2204
New York Islanders	80	31	38	11	73	281	288	1777
Pittsburgh Penguins	80	32	40	8	72	318	359	2132
Philadelphia Flyers	80	30	39	11	71	290	297	2067
Chicago Black Hawks	80	41	33	6	88	316	294	2426
St. Louis Blues	80	37	34	9	83	295	279	1809
Toronto Maple Leafs	80	38	38	4	80	337	358	2419
Minnesota North Stars	80	36	40	4	76	284	291	2041
Detroit Red Wings	80	28	38	14	70	288	323	2140
Calgary Flames	80	42	23	15	99	348	265	1751
Edmonton Oilers	80	38	28	14	90	315	283	2046

AMERICAN HORSE OF THE YEAR
ECLIPSE AWARD

Horse	Trainer	Owner	Age	Gender
Sunday Silence	Charlie Whittingham	H-G-W Partners	3	C

91

1990

NATIONAL FOOTBALL LEAGUE SEASON STANDINGS

EAST	W	L	T	WEST	W	L	T
Buffalo	13	3	0	LA Raiders	12	4	0
Miami	12	4	0	Kansas City	11	5	0
Indianapolis	7	9	0	Seattle	9	7	0
NY Jets	6	10	0	San Diego	6	10	0
New England	1	15	0	Denver	5	11	0
NY Giants	13	3	0	San Francisco	14	2	0
Philadelphia	10	6	0	New Orleans	8	8	0
Washington	10	6	0	LA Rams	5	11	0
Dallas	7	9	0	Atlanta	5	11	0

U.S BADMINTON CHAMPIONSHIPS WINNERS

Mens Singles	Womens Singles	Mens Doubles	Womens Doubles	Mixed Doubles
Chris Jogis	Linda Safarik-Tong	Chris Jogis Benny Lee	Ann French Joy Kitzmiller	Tom Reidy Traci Britton

NBA STANDINGS
DIVISION STANDINGS

Team	W	L	W/L%	GB	PS/G	PA/G	SRS
East							
Philadelphia 76ers	53	29	.646	–	110.2	105.2	4.23
Boston Celtics	52	30	.634	1.0	110.0	106.0	3.23
New York Knicks	45	37	.549	8.0	108.3	106.9	0.78
Washington Bullets	31	51	.378	22.0	107.7	109.9	-2.43
Miami Heat	18	64	.220	35.0	100.6	110.3	-9.59
New Jersey Nets	17	65	.207	36.0	100.1	108.0	-7.82
Detroit Pistons	59	23	.720	---	104.3	98.3	5.41
Chicago Bulls	55	27	.671	4.0	109.5	106.2	2.74
Milwaukee Bucks	44	38	.537	15.0	106.0	106.8	-1.06
Cleveland Cavaliers	42	40	.512	17.0	102.6	102.9	-0.62
Indiana Pacers	42	40	.512	17.0	109.3	109.1	-0.18
Atlanta Hawks	41	41	.500	18.0	108.5	107.5	0.64
Orlando Magic	18	64	.220	41.0	110.9	119.8	-8.73
West							
San Antonio Spurs	56	26	.683	---	106.3	102.8	3.58
Utah Jazz	55	27	.671	1.0	106.8	102.0	4.82

Dallas Mavericks	47	35	.573	9.0	102.2	102.2	0.42
Denver Nuggets	43	39	.524	13.0	114.6	113.2	1.56
Houston Rockets	41	41	.500	15.0	106.7	105.3	1.71
Minnesota Timberwolves	22	60	.268	34.0	95.2	99.4	-3.60
Charlotte Hornets	19	63	.232	37.0	100.4	108.2	-7.00
Los Angeles Lakers	63	19	.768	---	110.7	103.9	6.74
Portland Trail Blazers	59	23	.720	4.0	114.2	107.9	6.48
Phoenix Suns	54	28	.659	9.0	114.9	107.8	7.09
Seattle SuperSonics	41	41	.500	22.0	106.9	105.9	1.40
Golden State Warriors	37	45	.451	26.0	116.3	119.4	-2.55
Los Angeles Clippers	30	52	.366	33.0	103.8	107.2	-2.80
Sacramento Kings	23	59	.280	40.0	101.7	106.8	-4.41

AMERICAN HORSE OF THE YEAR
ECLIPSE AWARD

Horse	Trainer	Owner	Age	Gender
Criminal Type	D. Wayne Lukas	Calumet & Jurgen K. Arnemann	5	C

MAJOR LEAGUE BASEBALL SEASON HISTORY

American League Standings

TEAM	W	L	PCT	GB	HOME	ROAD	RS	RA	DIFF
Boston	88	74	.543	---	---	---	699	664	+35
Toronto	86	76	.531	2	---	---	767	661	+106
Detroit	79	83	.488	9	---	---	750	754	-4
Cleveland	77	85	.475	11	---	---	732	737	-5
Baltimore	76	85	.472	11.5	---	---	669	698	-29
Milwaukee	74	88	.457	14	---	---	732	760	-28
New York	67	95	.414	21	---	---	603	749	-146
Oakland	103	59	.636	---	---	---	733	570	+163
Chicago	94	68	.580	9	---	---	682	633	+49
Texas	83	79	.512	20	---	---	676	696	-20
California	80	82	.494	23	---	---	690	706	-16
Seattle	77	85	.475	26	---	---	640	680	-40
Kansas City	75	86	.466	27.5	---	---	707	709	-2698
Minnesota	84	88	.457	29	---	---	666	729	-63

National League Standings

TEAM	W	L	PCT	GB	HOME	ROAD	RS	RA	DIFF
Pittsburgh	95	67	.586	---	---	---	733	619	+114
New York	91	71	.562	4	---	---	775	613	+162
Montreal	85	77	.525	10	---	---	662	598	+64

93

Philadelphia	77	85	.475	18	---	---	646	729	-83
Chicago	77	85	.475	18	---	---	690	774	-84
St. Louis	70	92	.432	25	---	---	599	698	-99
Cincinnati	91	71	.562	---	---	---	693	597	+96
Los Angeles	86	76	.531	5	---	---	728	685	+43
San Francisco	85	77	.525	6	---	---	719	710	+9
San Diego	75	87	.463	16	---	---	673	673	0
Houston	75	87	.463	16	---	---	573	656	-83
Atlanta	65	97	.401	26	---	---	682	821	-139

U.S NATIONAL TENNIS CHAMPIONSHIPS

Mens Singles – Pete Sampras defeated Andre Agassi
Womens Singles – Gabriela Sabatini defeated Steffi Graf
Mens Doubles – Pieter Aldrich / Danie Viser defeated Paul Annacone / David Wheaton
Womens Doubles – Gigi Fernandez / Martina Navratilova defeated Jana Novotna / Helena Sukova
Mixed Doubles – Elizabeth Smylie / Todd Woodbridge defeated Natasha Zvereva / Jim Pugh

1991

NATIONAL FOOTBALL LEAGUE SEASON
STANDINGS

EAST	W	L	T	WEST	W	L	T
Buffalo	13	3	0	Denver	12	4	0
NY Jets	8	8	0	Kansas City	10	6	0
Miami	8	8	0	LA Raiders	9	7	0
New England	6	10	0	Seattle	7	9	0
Indianapolis	1	15	0	San Diego	4	12	0
Washington	14	2	0	New Orleans	11	5	0
Dallas	11	5	0	Atlanta	10	6	0
Philadelphia	10	6	0	San Francisco	10	6	0
NY Giants	8	8	0	LA Rams	3	13	0

U.S BADMINTON CHAMPIONSHIPS
WINNERS

Mens Singles	Womens Singles	Mens Doubles	Womens Doubles	Mixed Doubles
Chris Jogis	Liz Aronsohn	John Britton Tom Reidy	Ann French Joy Kitzmiller	Tariq Wadood Traci Britton

NBA STANDINGS
DIVISION STANDINGS

Team	W	L	W/L%	GB	PS/G	PA/G	SRS
East							
Boston Celtics	56	26	.683	-----	111.5	105.7	5.22
Philadelphia 76ers	44	38	.537	12.0	105.4	105.6	-0.39
New York Knicks	39	43	.476	17.0	103.1	103.3	-0.43
Washington Bullets	30	52	.366	26.0	101.4	106.4	-4.84
New Jersey Nets	26	56	.317	30.0	102.9	107.5	-4.53
Miami Heat	24	58	.293	32.0	101.8	107.8	-5.91
Chicago Bulls	61	21	.744	---	111.0	101.0	8.57
Detroit Pistons	50	32	.610	11.0	100.1	96.8	3.08
Milwaukee Bucks	48	34	.585	13.0	106.4	104.0	2.33
Atlanta Hawks	43	39	.524	18.0	109.8	109.0	0.72
Indiana Pacers	41	41	.500	20.0	111.7	112.1	-0.37
Cleveland Cavaliers	33	49	.402	28.0	101.7	104.2	-2.33
Charlotte Hornets	26	56	.317	35.0	102.8	108.0	-4.95
West							
San Antonio Spurs	55	27	.671	------	107.1	102.6	4.30
Utah Jazz	54	28	.659	1.0	104.0	100.7	3.18

Houston Rockets	52	30	.634	3.0	106.7	103.2	3.27
Orlando Magic	31	51	.378	24.0	105.9	109.9	-3.79
Minnesota Timberwolves	29	53	.354	26.0	99.6	103.5	-3.75
Dallas Mavericks	28	54	.341	27.0	99.9	104.5	-4.27
Denver Nugget	20	62	.244	35.0	119.9	130.8	-10.31
Portland Trail Blazers	63	19	.768	---	114.7	106.0	8.47
Los Angeles Lakers	58	24	.707	5.0	106.3	99.6	6.73
Phoenix Suns	55	27	.671	8.0	114.0	107.5	6.49
Golden State Warriors	44	38	.537	19.0	116.6	115.0	1.72
Seattle SuperSonics	41	41	.500	22.0	106.6	105.4	1.31
Los Angeles Clippers	31	51	.378	32.0	103.5	107.0	-3.16
Sacramento Kings	25	57	.305	38.0	96.7	103.5	-6.27

AMERICAN HORSE OF THE YEAR
ECLIPSE AWARD

Horse	Trainer	Owner	Age	Gender
Black Tie Affair	Ernie T. Poulos	Jeffrey Sullivan	5	C

NHL SEASON
FINAL STANDINGS

Wales / Campbell	GP	W	L	T	Pts	GF	GA	PIM
Montreal Canadiens	80	41	28	11	93	267	207	---
Boston Bruins	80	36	32	12	84	270	275	---
Buffalo Sabres	80	31	37	12	74	289	299	---
Hartford Whalers	80	26	41	13	65	247	283	---
Quebec Nordiques	80	20	48	12	52	255	318	---
New York Rangers	80	50	25	5	105	321	246	---
Washington Capitals	80	45	27	8	98	330	275	---
Pittsburgh Penguins	80	39	32	9	87	343	308	---
New Jersey Devils	80	38	31	11	87	289	259	---
New York Islanders	80	34	35	11	79	291	299	---
Philadelphia Flyers	80	32	37	11	75	252	273	---
Detroit Red Wings	80	43	25	12	98	320	256	---
Chicago Black Hawks	80	36	29	15	87	257	236	---
St. Louis Blues	80	36	33	11	83	279	266	---
Minnesota North Stars	80	32	42	6	70	246	278	---
Toronto Maple Leafs	80	30	43	7	67	234	294	---
Vancouver Canucks	80	42	26	12	96	285	250	---
Los Angeles Kings	80	35	31	14	84	287	296	---
Edmonton Oilers	80	36	34	10	82	295	297	---

1992

NATIONAL FOOTBALL LEAGUE SEASON
STANDINGS

EAST	W	L	T	WEST	W	L	T
Miami	11	5	0	San Diego	11	5	0
Buffalo	11	5	0	Kansas City	10	6	0
Indianapolis	9	7	0	Denver	8	8	0
NY Jets	4	12	0	LA Raiders	7	9	0
New England	2	14	0	Seattle	2	14	0
Dallas	13	3	0	San Francisco	14	2	0
Philadelphia	11	5	0	New Orleans	12	4	0
Washington	6	10	0	Atlanta	6	10	0
NY Giants	6	10	0	LA Rams	6	10	0

U.S BADMINTON CHAMPIONSHIPS
WINNERS

Mens Singles	Womens Singles	Mens Doubles	Womens Doubles	Mixed Doubles
Chris Jogis	Joy Kitzmiller	Benny Lee Tom Reidy	Ann French Joy Kitzmiller	Andy Chong Linda French

NBA STANDINGS
DIVISION STANDINGS

Team	W	L	W/L%	GB	PS/G	PA/G	SRS
East							
Boston Celtics	51	31	.622	–	106.6	103.0	3.41
New York Knicks	51	31	.622	---	101.6	97.7	3.67
New Jersey Nets	40	42	.488	11.0	105.4	107.1	-1.54
Miami Heat	38	44	.463	13.0	105.0	109.2	-3.94
Philadelphia 76ers	35	47	.427	16.0	101.9	103.2	-1.34
Washington Bullets	25	57	.305	26.0	102.4	106.8	-4.35
Orlando Magic	21	61	.256	30.0	101.6	108.5	-6.52
Chicago Bulls	67	15	.817	---	109.9	99.5	10.07
Cleveland Cavaliers	57	25	.695	10.0	108.9	103.4	5.34
Detroit Pistons	48	34	.585	19.0	98.9	96.9	2.06
Indiana Pacers	40	42	.488	27.0	112.1	110.3	1.85
Atlanta Hawks	38	44	.463	29.0	106.2	107.7	-1.15
Milwaukee Bucks	31	51	.378	36.0	105.0	106.7	-1.46
Charlotte Hornets	31	51	.378	36.0	109.5	113.4	-3.57
West							
Utah Jazz	55	27	.671	------	108.3	101.9	5.70

San Antonio Spurs	47	35	.573	8.0	104.0	100.6	2.81
Houston Rockets	42	40	.512	13.0	102.0	103.7	-1.94
Denver Nuggets	24	58	.293	31.0	99.7	107.6	-7.59
Dallas Mavericks	22	60	.268	33.0	97.6	105.3	-7.47
Minnesota Timberwolves	15	67	.183	40.0	100.5	107.5	-6.85
Portland Trail Blazers	57	25	.695	---	111.4	104.1	6.94
Golden State Warriors	55	27	.671	2.0	118.7	114.8	3.77
Phoenix Suns	53	29	.646	4.0	112.1	106.2	5.68
Seattle SuperSonics	47	35	.573	10.0	106.5	104.7	1.86
Los Angeles Clippers	45	37	.549	12.0	102.9	101.9	1.10
Los Angeles Lakers	43	39	.524	14.0	100.4	101.5	-0.95
Sacramento Kings	29	53	.354	28.0	104.3	110.3	-5.63

AMERICAN HORSE OF THE YEAR
ECLIPSE AWARD

Horse	Trainer	Owner	Age	Gender
A.P. Indy	Neil D. Drysdale	Tomonori Tsurumaki	3	C

NHL SEASON
FINAL STANDINGS

Prince of Wales / Clarence Campbell	GP	W	L	T	Pts	GF	GA	PIM
Boston Bruins	84	51	26	7	109	332	268	---
Quebec Nordiques	84	47	27	10	104	351	300	---
Montreal Canadiens	84	48	30	6	102	326	280	---
Buffalo Sabres	84	38	36	10	86	335	297	---
Hartford Whalers	84	26	52	6	58	284	369	---
Ottawa Senators	84	10	70	4	24	202	395	---
Pittsburgh Penguins	84	56	21	7	119	367	268	---
Washington Capitals	84	43	34	7	93	325	286	---
New York Islanders	84	40	37	7	87	335	297	---
New Jersey Devils	84	40	37	7	87	308	299	---
Philadelphia Flyers	84	36	37	11	83	319	319	---
New York Rangers	84	34	39	11	79	304	308	---
Chicago Black Hawks	84	47	25	12	106	279	230	---
Detroit Red Wings	84	47	28	9	103	369	280	---
Toronto Maple Leafs	84	44	29	11	99	288	241	---
St. Louis Blues	84	37	36	11	85	282	278	---
Minnesota North Stars	84	36	38	10	82	272	293	---
Tampa Bay Lightning	84	23	54	7	53	245	332	---
Vancouver Canucks	84	46	29	9	101	346	278	---

Calgary Flames	84	43	30	11	97	322	282	---
Los Angeles Kings	84	39	35	10	88	338	340	---
Winnipeg Jets	84	40	37	7	87	322	320	---
Edmonton Oilers	84	26	50	8	60	242	337	---
San Jose Sharks	84	11	71	2	24	218	414	---

MAJOR LEAGUE BASEBALL SEASON HISTORY

American League Standings

TEAM	W	L	PCT	GB	HOME	ROAD	RS	RA	DIFF
Torontoo	99	66	.593	---	---	---	780	682	+98
Milwaukee	92	70	.568	4	---	---	740	604	+136
Baltimore	89	73	.549	7	---	---	705	656	+49
New York	76	86	.469	20	---	---	733	746	-13
Cleveland	76	86	.469	20	---	---	674	746	-72
Detroit	75	87	.463	21	---	---	791	794	-3
Boston	73	89	.451	23	---	---	599	669	-70
Oakland	96	66	.593	---	---	---	745	672	+73
Minnesota	90	72	.556	6	---	---	747	653	+94
Chicago	86	76	.531	10	---	---	738	690	+48
Texas	77	85	.475	19	---	---	682	753	-71
Kansas City	72	90	.444	24	---	---	610	667	-57
California	72	90	.444	24	---	---	579	671	-92
Seattle	64	98	.395	32	---	---	679	799	-120

National League Standings

TEAM	W	L	PCT	GB	HOME	ROAD	RS	RA	DIFF
Pittsburgh	96	66	.593	---	---	---	693	595	+98
Montreal	87	75	.537	9	---	---	648	581	+67
St. Louis	83	79	.512	13	---	---	631	604	+27
Chicago	78	84	.481	18	---	---	593	624	-31
New York	72	90	.444	24	---	---	599	653	-54
Philadelphia	70	92	.432	26	---	---	686	717	-31
Atlanta	98	64	.605	---	---	---	682	569	+113
Cincinnati	90	72	.556	8	---	---	660	609	+51
San Diego	82	80	.506	16	---	---	617	636	-19
Houston	81	81	.500	17	---	---	608	668	-60
San Francisco	72	90	.444	26	---	---	574	647	-73
Los Angeles	63	99	.389	35	---	---	548	636	-88

1993

NATIONAL FOOTBALL LEAGUE SEASON STANDINGS

EAST	W	L	T	WEST	W	L	T
Buffalo	12	4	0	Kansas City	11	5	0
Miami	9	7	0	LA Raiders	10	6	0
NY Jets	8	8	0	Denver	9	7	0
New England	5	11	0	San Diego	8	8	0
Indianapolis	4	12	0	Seattle	6	10	0
Dallas	12	4	0	San Francisco	10	6	0
NY Giants	11	5	0	New Orleans	8	8	0
Philadelphia	8	8	0	Atlanta	6	10	0
Phoenix	7	9	0	LA Rams	5	11	0

U.S BADMINTON CHAMPIONSHIPS WINNERS

Mens Singles	Womens Singles	Mens Doubles	Womens Doubles	Mixed Doubles
Andy Chong	Andrea Andersson	Benny Lee Tom Reidy	Andrea Andersson Traci Britton	Andy Chong Linda French

NBA STANDINGS DIVISION STANDINGS

Team	W	L	W/L%	GB	PS/G	PA/G	SRS
East							
New York Knicks	60	22	.732	–	101.6	95.4	5.87
Boston Celtics	48	34	.585	12.0	103.7	102.8	0.93
New Jersey Nets	43	39	.524	17.0	102.8	101.6	1.20
Orlando Magic	41	41	.500	19.0	105.5	104.2	1.35
Miami Heat	36	46	.439	24.0	103.6	104.7	-0.93
Philadelphia 76ers	26	56	.317	34.0	104.3	110.1	-5.25
Washington Bullets	22	60	.268	38.0	101.9	108.9	-6.49
Chicago Bulls	57	25	.695	---	105.2	98.9	6.19
Cleveland Cavaliers	54	28	.659	3.0	107.7	101.3	6.30
Charlotte Hornets	44	38	.537	13.0	110.1	110.4	-0.02
Atlanta Hawks	43	39	.524	14.0	107.5	108.4	-0.67
Indiana Pacers	41	41	.500	16.0	107.8	106.1	1.77
Detroit Pistons	40	42	.488	17.0	100.6	102.0	-1.10
Milwaukee Bucks	28	54	.341	29.0	102.3	106.1	-3.26
West							
Houston Rockets	55	27	.671	------	104.0	99.8	3.57

San Antonio Spurs	49	33	.598	6.0	105.5	102.8	2.21
Utah Jazz	47	35	.573	8.0	106.2	104.0	1.74
Denver Nuggets	36	46	.439	19.0	105.2	106.9	-2.14
Minnesota Timberwolves	19	63	.232	36.0	98.1	105.9	-7.62
Dallas Mavericks	11	71	.134	44.0	99.3	114.5	-14.68
Phoenix Suns	62	20	.756	---	113.4	106.7	6.27
Seattle SuperSonics	55	27	.671	7.0	108.3	101.3	6.66
Portland Trail Blazers	51	31	.622	11.0	108.5	105.4	2.92
Los Angeles Clippers	41	41	.500	21.0	107.1	106.8	0.33
Los Angeles Lakers	39	43	.476	23.0	104.2	105.5	-1.20
Golden State Warriors	34	48	.415	28.0	109.9	110.9	-0.94
Sacramento Kings	25	57	.305	37.0	107.9	111.1	-3.00

AMERICAN HORSE OF THE YEAR
ECLIPSE AWARD

Horse	Trainer	Owner	Age	Gender
Kotashaan	Richard Mandella	La Presle Farm	5	C

U.S NATIONAL TENNIS CHAMPIONSHIPS

Mens Singles – Pete Sampras defeated Cedric Pioline
Womens Singles – Steffi Graf defeated Helena Sukova
Mens Doubles – Ken Flach / Rick Leach defeated Karel Novacek / Martin Damm
Womens Doubles – Arantxa Sanchez Vicario / Helena Sukova defeated Amanda Coetzer / Ines Gorrochategui
Mixed Doubles – Helena Sukova / Todd Woodbridge defeated Martina Navatilova / Mark Woodforde

101

1994

NATIONAL FOOTBALL LEAGUE SEASON STANDINGS

EAST	W	L	T	WEST	W	L	T
Miami	10	6	0	San Diego	11	5	0
New England	10	6	0	Kansas City	9	7	0
Indianapolis	8	8	0	LA Raider	9	7	0
Buffalo	7	9	0	Denver	7	9	0
NY Jets	6	10	0	Seattle	6	10	0
Dallas	12	4	0	San Francisco	13	3	0
NY Giants	9	7	0	New Orleans	7	9	0
Arizona	8	8	0	Atlanta	7	9	0
Philadelphia	7	9	0	LA Rams	4	12	0
Washington	3	13	0				

U.S BADMINTON CHAMPIONSHIPS WINNERS

Mens Singles	Womens Singles	Mens Doubles	Womens Doubles	Mixed Doubles
Kevin Han	Joy Kitzmiller	Benny Lee Tom Reidy	Andrea Andersson Liz Aronsohn	Andy Chong Linda French

NBA STANDINGS
DIVISION STANDINGS

Team	W	L	W/L%	GB	PS/G	PA/G	SRS
East							
New York Knicks	57	25	.695	–	98.5	91,5	6.48
Orlando Magic	50	32	.610	7.0	105.7	101.8	3.68
New Jersey Nets	45	37	.549	12.0	103.2	101.0	2.11
Miami Heat	42	40	.512	15.0	103.4	100.7	2.40
Boston Celtics	32	50	.390	25.0	100.8	105.1	-4.28
Philadelphia 76ers	25	57	.305	32.0	98.0	105.6	-7.37
Washington Bullets	24	58	.293	33.0	100.4	107.7	-7.13
Atlanta Hawks	57	25	.695	---	101.4	96.2	4.94
Chicago Bulls	55	27	.671	2.0	98.0	94.9	2.87
Indiana Pacers	47	35	.573	10.0	101.0	97.5	3.26
Cleveland Cavaliers	47	35	.573	10.0	101.2	97.1	3.64
Charlotte Hornets	41	41	.500	16.0	106.5	106.7	-0.23
Milwaukee Bucks	20	62	.244	37.0	96.9	103.4	-6.24
Detroit Pistons	20	62	.244	37.0	96.9	104.7	-7.46

West

Houston Rockets	58	24	.707	---	101.1	96.8	4.19
San Antonio Spurs	55	27	.671	3.0	100.0	94.8	5.05
Utah Jazz	53	29	.646	5.0	101.9	97.7	4.10
Denver Nuggets	42	40	.512	16.0	100.3	98.8	1.54
Minnesota Timberwolves	20	62	.244	38.0	96.7	103.6	-6.55
Dallas Mavericks	13	69	.159	45.0	95.1	103.8	-8.19
Seattle SuperSonics	63	19	.768	---	105.9	96.9	8.68
Phoenix Suns	56	26	.683	7.0	108.2	103.4	4.68
Golden State Warriors	50	32	.610	13.0	107.9	106.1	1.76
Portland Trail Blazers	47	35	.573	16.0	107.3	104.6	2.60
LA Lakers	33	49	.402	30.0	100.4	104.7	-3.93
Sacramento Kings	28	54	.341	35.0	101.1	106.9	-5.32
Los Angeles Clippers	27	55	.329	36.0	103.0	108.7	-5.28

AMERICAN HORSE OF THE YEAR
ECLIPSE AWARD

Horse	Trainer	Owner	Age	Gender
Holy Bull	Warren A. Croll, Jr	Warren A. Croll, Jr	3	C

U.S NATIONAL TENNIS CHAMPIONSHIPS

Mens Singles – Andre Agassi defeated Michael Stich
Womens Singles – Arantxa Sanchez Vicario defeated Steffi Graf
Mens Doubles – Jacco Eltingh / Paul Haarhuis defeated Todd Woodbridge / Mark Woodforde
Womens Doubles – Jana Novotna / Arantxa Sanchez Vicarioo defeated Katerina Maleeva / Robin White
Mixed Doubles – Elna Reinach / Patrick Galbraith defeated Jana Novotna / Todd Wooodbridge

103

1995

NATIONAL FOOTBALL LEAGUE SEASON STANDINGS

EAST	W	L	T	WEST	W	L	T
Buffalo	10	6	0	Kansas City	13	3	0
Indianapolis	9	7	0	San Diego	9	7	0
Miami	9	7	0	Seattle	8	8	0
New England	6	10	0	Denver	8	8	0
NY Jets	3	13	0	Oakland	8	8	0
Dallas	12	4	0	San Francisco	11	5	0
Philadelphia	10	6	0	Atlanta	9	7	0
Washington	6	10	0	St. Louis	7	9	0
NY Giants	5	11	0	New Orleans	7	9	0
Arizona	4	12	0	Carolina	7	9	0

U.S BADMINTON CHAMPIONSHIPS WINNERS

Mens Singles	Womens Singles	Mens Doubles	Womens Doubles	Mixed Doubles
Kevin Han	Andrea Andersson	Benny Lee Tom Reidy	Andrea Andersson Liz Aronsohn	Andy Chong Linda French

NBA STANDINGS
DIVISION STANDINGS

Team	W	L	W/L%	GB	PS/G	PA/G	SRS
East							
Orlando Magic	57	25	.695	-----	110.9	103.8	6.44
New York Knicks	55	27	.671	2.0	98.2	95.1	2.78
Boston Celtics	35	47	.427	22.0	102.8	104.7	-1.92
Miami Heat	32	50	.390	25.0	101.1	102.8	-1.85
New Jersey Nets	30	52	.366	27.0	98.1	101.2	-3.28
Philadelphia 76ers	24	58	.293	33.0	95.4	100.4	-5.06
Washington Bullets	21	61	.256	36.0	100.5	106.1	-5.56
Indiana Pacers	52	30	.634	---	99.2	95.5	3.35
Charlotte Hornets	50	32	.610	2.0	100.6	97.3	2.87
Chicago Bulls	47	35	.573	5.0	101.5	86.7	4.23
Cleveland Cavaliers	43	39	.524	9.0	90.5	89.8	0.55
Atlanta Hawks	42	40	.512	10.0	96.6	95.3	1.06
Milwaukee Bucks	34	48	.415	18.0	99.3	103.7	-4.30
Detroit Pistons	28	54	.341`	24.0	98.2	105.5	-7.08

West

San Antonio Spurs	62	20	.756	---	106.6	100.6	5.90
Utah Jazz	60	22	.732	2.0	106.4	98.4	7.76
Houston Rockets	47	35	.573	15.0	103.5	101.4	2.32
Denver Nuggets	41	41	.500	21.0	101.3	100.5	0.96
Dallas Mavericks	36	46	.439	26.0	103.2	106.1	-2.39
Minnesota Timberwolves	21	61	.256	41.0	94.2	103.2	-8.22
Phoenix Suns	59	23	.720	---	110.6	106.8	3.86
Seattle SuperSonics	57	25	.695	2.0	110.4	102.2	7.91
Los Angeles Lakers	48	34	.585	11.0	105.1	105.3	-0.01
Portland Trail Blazers	44	38	.537	15.0	103.1	99.2	3.80
Sacramento Kings	39	43	.476	20.0	98.2	99.2	-0.74
Golden State Warriors	26	56	.317	33.0	105.7	111.1	-4.90
Los Angeles Clippers	17	65	.207	242.0	96.7	105.8	-8.43

AMERICAN HORSE OF THE YEAR
ECLIPSE AWARD

Horse	Trainer	Owner	Age	Gender
Cigar	William I. Mott	Allen E. Paulson	5	C

1995 U.S NATIOONOAL TENNIS CHAMPIONSHIPS

Mens Singles – Pete Sampras defeated Andre Agassi
Womens Singles – Steffi Graf defeated Monica Seles
Mens Doubles – Tod Woodforde / Mark Woodforde defeated Alex O'Brien / Sandon Stolle
Womens Doubles – Gigi Fernandez / Natasha Zvereva defeated Brenda Schiltz-McCarthy / Rennae Stubbs
Mixed Doubles – Meredith McGrath / Matt Lucena defeated Gigi Fernandez / Cyriil Suk

1996

NATIONAL FOOTBALL LEAGUE SEASON STANDINGS

EAST	W	L	T	WEST	W	L	T
New England	11	5	0	Denver	13	3	0
Buffalo	10	6	0	Kansas City	9	7	0
Indianapolis	9	7	0	San Diego	8	8	0
Miami	8	8	0	Oakland	7	9	0
NY Jets	1	15	0	Seattle	7	9	0
Dallas	10	6	0	Carolina	12	4	0
Philadelphia	10	6	0	San Francisco	12	4	0
Washington	9	7	0	St. Louis	6	10	0
Arizona	7	9	0	Atlanta	3	13	0
NY Giants	6	10	0	New Orleans	3	13	0

U.S BADMINTON CHAMPIONSHIPS WINNERS

Mens Singles	Womens Singles	Mens Doubles	Womens Doubles	Mixed Doubles
Steve Butler	Zhao Ye Ping	Kevin Han Tom Reidy	Ann French Kathy Zimmerman	Andy Chong Zhao Ye Ping

NBA STANDINGS DIVISION STANDINGS

Team	W	L	W/L%	GB	PS/G	PA/G	SRS
East							
Orlando Magic	60	22	.732	-----	104.5	99.0	5.40
New York Knicks	47	35	.573	13.0	97.2	94.9	2.24
Miami Heat	42	40	.512	18.0	96.5	95.0	1.46
Washington Bullets	39	43	.476	21.0	102.5	101.5	0.99
Boston Celtics	33	49	.402	27.0	103.6	107.0	-3.37
New York Nets	30	52	.366	30.0	93.7	97.9	-4.14
Philadelphia 76ers	18	64	.220	42.0	94.5	104.5	-9.45
Chicago Bulls	72	10	.878	---	105.2	92.9	11.80
Indiana Pacers	52	30	.634	20.0	99.3	96.1	3.11
Cleveland Cavaliers	47	35	.573	25.0	91.1	88.5	2.49
Atlanta Hawks	46	36	.561	26.0	98.3	97.1	1.29
Detroit Pistons	46	36	.561	26.0	95.4	92.9	2.45
Charlotte Hornets	41	41	.500	31.0	102.8	103.4	-0.48
Milwaukee Bucks	25	57	.305	47.0	95.6	100.9	-4.92
Toronto Raptors	21	61	.256	51.0	97.5	105.0	-7.20

West

San Antonio Spurs	59	23	.720	---	103.4	97.1	5.98
Utah Jazz	55	27	.671	4.0	102.5	95.9	6.25
Houston Rockets	48	34	.585	11.0	102.5	100.7	1.63
Denver Nuggets	35	47	.427	24.0	97.7	100.4	-2.62
Minnesota Timberwolves	26	56	.317	33.0	97.9	103.2	-5.14
Dallas Mavericks	26	56	.317	33.0	102.5	107.5	-4.71
Vancouver Grizzlies	15	67	.183	44.0	89.8	99.8	-9.55
Seattle SuperSonics	64	18	.780	---	104.5	96.7	7.40
Los Angeles Lakers	53	29	.646	11.0	102.9	98.5	4.21
Portland Trail Blazers	44	38	.537	20.0	99.3	97.0	2.21
Phoenix Suns	41	41	.500	23.0	104.3	104.0	0.28
Sacramento Kings	39	43	.476	25.0	99.5	102.3	-2.62
Golden State Warriors	36	46	.439	28.0	101.6	103.1	-1.42
Los Angeles Clippers	29	53	.354	35.0	99.4	103.0	-3.46

AMERICAN HORSE OF THE YEAR
ECLIPSE AWARD

Horse	Trainer	Owner	Age	Gender
Cigar	William I. Mott	Allen E. Paulson	6	C

NHL SEASON
FINAL STANDINGS

Teams	W	L	T	GF	GA	Pts	---	---
Buffalo Sabres	40	30	12	237	208	92		
Pittsburgh Pen6guins	38	36	8	285	280	84		
Ottawa Senators	31	36	15	249	276	77		
Montreal Canadiens	31	36	15	249	276	77		
Hartford Whalers	32	39	11	226	256	75		
Boston Bruins	26	47	9	234	300	61		
New Jersey Devils	45	23	14	231	182	104		
Philadelphia Flyers	45	24	13	274	217	103		
Florida Panthers	35	28	19	221	201	89		
New York Rangers	38	34	10	258	231	86		
Washington Capitals	33	40	9	214	231	75		
Tampa Bay Lightning	32	40	10	217	247	74		
New York Islanders	29	41	12	240	250	70		
Dallas Stars	48	26	8	252	198	104		
Detroit Red Wings	38	26	18	253	197	94		
Phoenix Coyotes	38	37	7	240	243	83		

St. Louis Blues	36	35	11	236	239	83		
Chicago Black Hawks	34	35	13	223	210	81		
Toronto Maple Leafs	30	44	8	230	273	68		
Colorado Avalanche	49	24	9	277	205	107		
Mighty Ducks of Anaheim	36	33	13	243	231	85		
Edmonton Oilers	36	37	9	252	247	81		
Vancouver Canucks	35	40	7	257	273	77		
Calgary Flames	32	41	9	214	239	73		
Los Angeles Kings	28	43	11	214	268	67		
San Jose Sharks	27	47	8	211	278	62		

U.S NATIONAL TENNIS CHAMPIONSHIPS

Mens Singles – Pete Sampras defeated Michael Chang
Womens Singles – Steffi Graf defeated Monica Seles
Mens Doubles – Todd Woodbridge / Mark Woodforde defeated Jacco Eltingh / Paul Haarhuis
Womens Doubles – Gigi Fernandez / Natasha Zvereva defeated Jana Novotna / Arantxa Sanchez Vicario
Mixed Doubles – Lisa Raymond / Patrick Galbraith defeated Manon Bollegraf / Rick Leach

108

1997

NATIONAL FOOTBALL LEAGUE SEASON
STANDINGS

EAST	W	L	T	WEST	W	L	T
New England	10	6	0	Kansas City	13	3	0
Miami	9	7	0	Denver	12	4	0
NY Jets	9	7	0	Seattle	8	8	0
Buffalo	6	10	0	Oakland	4	12	0
Indianapolis	3	13	0	San Diego	4	12	0
NY Giants	10	5	1	San Francisco	13	3	0
Washington	8	7	0	Carolina	7	9	0
Philadelphia	6	9	1	Atlanta	7	9	0
Dallas	6	10	0	New Orleans	6	10	0
Arizona	4	12	0	St. Louis	5	11	0

U.S BADMINTON CHAMPIONSHIPS
WINNERS

Mens Singles	Womens Singles	Mens Doubles	Womens Doubles	Mixed Doubles
Kevin Han	Cindy Shi	Kevin Han Tom Reidy	Cindy Shi Zhao Ye Ping	Trisna Gunadi Eileen Tang

NBA STANDINGS
DIVISION STANDINGS

Team	W	L	W/L%	GB	PS/G	PA/G	SRS
East							
Miami Heat	61	21	.744	–	94.8	89.3	5.56
New York Knicks	57	25	.695	4.0	95.4	92.2	3.31
Orlando Magic	45	37	.549	16.0	94.1	94.5	-0.07
Washington Bullets	44	38	.537	17.0	99.4	97.7	1.77
Philadelphia 76ers	22	60	.268	39.0	100.2	106.7	-5.89
Boston Celtics	15	67	.183	46.0	100.6	107.9	-6.62
Chicago Bulls	69	13	.841	---	103.1	92.3	10.70
Atlanta Hawks	56	26	.683	13.0	94.8	89.4	5.52
Detroit Pistons	54	28	.659	15.0	94.2	88.9	5.45
Charlotte Hornets	54	28	.659	15.0	98.9	97.0	2.13
Cleveland Cavaliers	42	40	.512	27.0	87.5	85.6	2.32
Indiana Pacers	39	43	.476	30.0	95.4	94.4	1.49
Milwaukee Bucks	33	49	.402	36.0	95.3	97.2	-1.38
Toronto Raptors	30	52	.366	39.0	95.5	98.6	-2.56

West

Utah Jazz	64	18	.780	---	103.1	94.3	7.97
Houston Rockets	57	25	.695	7.0	100.6	96.1	3.85
Minnesota Timberwolves	40	42	.488	24.0	96.1	97.6	-1.82
Dallas Mavericks	24	58	.293	40.0	90.6	97.0	-6.47
Denver Nuggets	21	61	.256	43.0	97.8	104.1	-6.40
San Antonio Spurs	20	62	.244	44.0	90.5	98.3	-7.93
Vancouver Grizzlies	14	68	.171	50.0	89.2	99.4	-10.17
Seattle SuperSonics	57	25	.695	---	100.9	93.2	6.91
Los Angeles Lakers	56	26	.683	1.0	100.0	95.7	3.66
Portland Trail Blazers	49	33	.598	8.0	99.0	94.8	3.56
Phoenix Suns	40	42	.488	17.0	102.8	102.2	0.21
Los Angeles Clippers	36	46	.439	21.0	97.2	99.5	-2.66
Sacramento Kings	34	48	.415	23.0	96.4	99.8	-3.64
Golden State Warriors	30	52	.366	27.0	99.6	104.4	-4.90

AMERICAN HORSE OF THE YEAR
ECLIPSE AWARD

Horse	Trainer	Owner	Age	Gender
Favorite Trick	Patrick B. Byrne	Joseph LaCombe	2	C

NHL SEASON
FINAL STANDINGS

Team	W	L	T	GF	GA	Pts	---	---
Pittsburgh Penguins	40	24	18	228	188	98		
Boston Bruins	39	30	13	221	194	91		
Buffalo Sabres	36	29	17	211	187	89		
Montreal Canadiens	37	32	13	235	208	87		
Ottawa Senators	34	33	15	193	200	83		
Carolina Hurricanes	33	41	8	200	219	74		
New Jersey Devils	48	23	11	225	166	107		
Philadelphia Flyers	42	29	11	242	193	95		
Washington Capitals	40	30	12	219	202	92		
New York Islanders	30	41	11	212	225	71		
New York Rangers	25	39	18	197	231	68		
Florida Panthers	24	43	15	203	256	63		
Tampa Bay Lightning	17	55	10	151	269	44		
Dallas Stars	49	22	11	242	167	109		
Detroit Red Wings	44	23	15	250	196	103		
St. Louis Blues	45	29	8	256	204	98		

110

Phoenix Coyotes	35	35	12	224	227	82
Chicago Black Hawks	30	39	13	192	199	73
Toronto Maple Leafs	30	43	9	194	237	69
Colorado Avalanche	39	26	17	231	205	95
Los Angeles Kings	38	33	11	227	225	87
Edmonton Oilers	35	37	10	215	224	80
San Jose Sharks	34	38	10	210	216	78
Calgary Flames	26	41	15	217	252	67
Mighty Ducks of Anaheim	26	43	13	205	261	65
Vancouver Canucks	25	43	14	224	273	64

U.S NATIONAL TENNIS CHAMPIONSHIPS

Mens Singles – Patrick Rafter defeated Greg Rusedski
Womens Singles – Martina Hingis defeated Venus Williams
Mens Doubles – Yevgeny Kafelnikov / Daniel Vacek defeated Jonas Bjorkman / Nicklas Kulti
Womens Doubles – Lindsay Davenport / Jana Novotna defeated Gigi Fernandez / Natasha Zvereva
Mixed Doubles – Manon Bollegraf / Rich Leach defeated Mercedes Paz / Pablo Albano

111

1998

NATIONAL FOOTBALL LEAGUE SEASON
STANDINGS

EAST	W	L	T	WEST	W	L	T
NY Jets	12	4	0	Denver	14	2	0
Miami	10	6	0	Oakland	8	8	0
Buffalo	10	6	0	Seattle	8	8	0
New England	9	7	0	Kansas City	7	9	0
Indianapolis	3	13	0	San Diego	5	11	0
Dallas	10	6	0	Atlanta	14	2	0
Arizona	9	7	0	San Francisco	12	4	0
NY Giants	8	8	0	New Orleans	6	10	0
Washington	6	10	0	Carolina	4	12	0
Philadelphia	3	13	0	St. Louis	4	12	0

U.S BADMINTON CHAMPIONSHIPS
WINNERS

Mens Singles	Womens Singles	Mens Doubles	Womens Doubles	Mixed Doubles
Kevin Han	Yeping Tang	Andy Chong Benny Lee	Cindy Shi Yeping Tang	Andy Chong Yeping Tang

AMERICAN HORSE OF THE YEAR
ECLIPSE AWARD

Horse	Trainer	Owner	Age	Gender
Skip Away	Sonny Hine	Carolyne Hine	5	C

NHL SEASON
FINAL STANDINGS

Team	GP	W	L	T	Pts	GF	GA	PIM
New Jersey Devils	82	47	24	11	105	248	196	1355
Philadelphia Flyers	82	37	26	19	93	231	196	1075
Pittsburgh Penguins	82	38	30	14	90	242	225	977
New York Rangers	82	33	38	11	77	217	227	1087
New York Islanders	82	24	48	10	58	194	244	1111
Ottawa Senators	82	44	23	15	103	239	179	892
Toronto Maple Leafs	82	45	30	7	97	268	231	1095
Boston Bruins	82	39	30	13	91	214	181	1182
Buffalo Sabers	82	37	28	17	91	207	175	1561
Montreal Canadiens	82	32	39	11	75	184	209	1299
Carolina Hurricanes	82	34	30	18	86	210	202	1158
Florida Panthers	82	30	34	18	78	210	228	1522

Team	GP	W	L	OTL	PTS	GF	GA	PIM
Washington Capitals	82	31	45	6	68	200	218	1381
Detroit Red Wings	82	43	32	7	93	245	202	1202
St. Louis Blues	82	37	32	13	87	237	209	1308
Chicago Black Hawks	82	29	41	12	70	202	248	1807
Nashville Predators	82	28	47	7	63	190	261	1420
Colorado Avalanche	82	44	28	10	98	239	205	1619
Edmonton Oilers	82	33	37	12	78	230	226	1373
Calgary Flames	82	30	40	12	72	211	234	1389
Vancouver Canucks	82	23	47	12	58	192	258	1764
Dallas Stars	82	51	19	12	114	236	168	1108
Phoenix Coyotes	82	39	31	12	90	205	197	1412
Anaheim Mighty Ducks	82	35	34	13	83	215	206	1323
San Jose Sharks	82	31	33	18	80	196	191	1423
Los Angeles Kings	82	32	45	5	69	189	222	1383

U.S NATIONAL TENNIS CHAMPIONSHIPS

Mens Singles – Patrick Rafter defeated Mark Philippoussis
Womens Singles – Lindsay Davenport deafeated Martina Hingis
Mens Doubles – Sandon Stolle / Cyril Suk defeated Mark Knowles
Womens Doubles – Martina Hingis / Jana Noovotna defeated Lindsay Davenport / Natasha Zvereva
Mixed Doubles – Serena Williams / Max Mirnyi defeared Lisa Raymond / Patrick Galbraith

1999-2000

NATIONAL FOOTBALL LEAGUE SEASON
STANDINGS

EAST	W	L	T	WEST	W	L	T
Indianapolis	13	3	0	Seattle	9	7	0
Buffalo	11	5	0	Kansas City	9	7	0
Miami	9	7	0	San Diego	8	8	0
NY Jets	8	8	0	Oakland	8	8	0
New England	8	8	0	Denver	6	10	0
Washington	10	6	0	St. Louis	13	3	0
Dallas	8	8	0	Carolina	8	8	0
NY Giant	7	9	0	Atlanta	5	11	0
Arizona	6	10	0	San Francisco	4	12	0
Philadelphia	5	11	0	New Orleans	3	13	0

U.S BADMINTON CHAMPIONSHIPS
WINNERS

Mens Singles	Womens Singles	Mens Doubles	Womens Doubles	Mixed Doubles
Kevin Han	Yeping Tang	Kevin Han Alex Liang	Cindy Shi Yeping Tang	Andy Chong Yeping Tang

AMERICAN HORSE OF THE YEAR
ECLIPSE AWARD

Horse	Trainer	Owner	Age	Gender
Charismatic	D. Wyne Lukas	Bob and Beverly Lewis	3	C

NHL SEASON
FINAL STANDINGS

Team	GP	W	L	T	Pts	GF	GA	PIM
Toronto Maple Leafs	82	45	27	7	100	246	222	1103
Ottawa Senators	82	41	28	11	95	244	210	850
Buffalo Sabres	82	35	32	11	85	213	204	1173
Montreal Canadiens	82	35	34	9	83	196	194	1067
Boston Bruins	82	24	33	19	73	210	248	865
Philadelphia Flyers	82	45	22	12	105	237	179	1233
New Jersey Devils	82	45	24	8	103	251	203	1313
Pittsburgh Penguins	82	37	31	8	88	241	236	1221
New York Rangers	82	29	38	12	73	218	246	916
New York Islanders	82	24	48	9	58	194	275	1376
Washington Capitals	82	44	24	12	102	227	194	994
Florida Panthers	82	43	27	6	98	244	209	1329

Carolina Hurricanes	82	37	35	10	84	217	216	799
Tampa Bay Lightning	82	19	47	9	54	204	310	1733
Atlanta Thrashers	82	14	57	7	39	170	313	1422
St. Louis Blues	82	51	19	11	114	248	165	1139
Detroit Red Wings	82	48	22	10	108	278	210	1014
Chicago Black Hawks	82	33	37	10	78	242	245	1444
Nashville Predators	82	28	40	7	70	199	240	946
Dallas Stars	82	43	23	10	102	211	184	1029
Los Angeles Kings	82	39	27	12	94	245	228	1313
Phoenix Coyotes	82	39	31	8	90	232	228	940
San Jose Sharks	82	35	30	10	87	225	214	1292
Mighty Ducks of Anaheim	82	34	33	12	83	217	227	926
Colorado Avalanche	82	42	28	11	96	233	201	1118
Edmonton Oilers	82	32	26	16	88	226	212	1344
Vancouver Canucks	82	30	29	15	83	227	237	1047
Calgary Flames	82	31	36	10	77	211	256	1267

MAJOR LEAGUE BASEBALL SEASON HISTORY

American League Standings

TEAM	W	L	PCT	GB	HOME	ROAD	RS	RA	DIFF
New York	98	64	.605	---	48-33	50-31	900	731	+169
Boston	94	68	.580	4	49-32	45-36	836	718	+118
Toronto	84	78	.519	14	40-41	44-37	883	862	+21
Baltimore	78	84	.481	20	41-40	37-44	851	815	+36
Tampa Bay	69	93	.426	29	33-48	36-45	772	913	-141
Cleveland	97	65	.599	---	47-34	50-31	1009	860	+149
Chicago	75	86	.466	21.5	38-42	37-44	777	870	-93 ·
Detroit	69	92	.429	27.5	38-43	31-49	747	882	-135
Kansas City	64	97	.398	32.5	33-47	31-50	856	921	-65
Minnesota	63	97	.394	33	31-50	32-47	686	845	-159
Texas	95	67	.586	---	51-30	44-37	945	859	+86
Oakland	87	75	.537	8	52-29	35-46	839	846	+47
Seattle	79	83	.488	16	43-38	36-45	859	905	-46
Anaheim	70	92	.432	25	37-44	33-48	711	826	-115

National League Standings

TEAM	W	L	PCT	GB	HOME	ROAD	RS	RA	DIFF
Atlanta	103	59	.636	---	56-25	47-34	840	661	+179
New York	97	66	.595	6.5	49-32	48-34	853	711	+142
Philadelphia	77	85	.475	26	41-40	36-45	841	846	-5

115

Montreal	68	94	.420	35	35-46	33-48	718	853	-135
Florida	64	98	.395	39	35-45	29-53	691	852	-161
Houston	97	65	.599	---	50-32	47-33	823	675	+148
Cincinnati	96	67	.589	1.5	45-37	51-30	865	711	+154
Pittsburgh	78	83	.484	18.5	45-36	33-47	775	782	-7
St. Louis	75	86	.466	21.5	38-42	37-44	809	838	-29
Milwaukee	74	87	.460	22.5	32-48	42-39	815	886	-71
Chicago	67	95	.414	30	34-47	33-48	747	920	-173
Arizona	100	62	.617	---	52-29	48-33	908	676	+232
San Francisco	86	76	.531	14	49-32	37-44	872	831	+41
Los Angeles	77	85	.475	23	37-44	40-41	793	787	+6
San Diego	74	88	.457	26	46-35	28-53	710	781	-71
Colorado	72	90	.444	28	39-42	33-48	906	1028	-122

U.S NATIONAL TENNIS CHAMPIONSHIPS

Mens Singles – Andre Agassi defeated Todd Martin
Womens Singles – Serena Williams defeated Martina Hingis
Mens Doubles – Sebastien Lareau / Alex O'Brien defeated Mahesh Bhupathi / Leander Paes
Womens Doubles – Serena Williams / Venus Williams defeated Chanda Rubin / Sandrine Testud
Mixed Doubles – Ai Sugiyama / Mahesh Bhupathi defeated Kimberley Po / Donald Johnson

Made in the USA
Coppell, TX
31 January 2022

72729601R00075